THE DECORATED DIAGRAM

The MIT Press
Cambridge, Massachusetts
London, England

THE DECORATED DIAGRAM

Harvard Architecture and

the Failure of the Bauhaus Legacy

Klaus Herdeg

November 1983

This book was set in Linotron 202 Frutiger by DEKR Corporation and printed and bound by The Murray Printing Company in the United States of America.

Library of Congress Cataloging in Publication Data

Herdeg, Klaus.
  The decorated diagram.

  Includes index.
    1. Architecture, Modern—20th century—United States.
2. Architecture—United States. 3. Gropius, Walter,
1833–1969—Influence. 4. Harvard University. Graduate
School of Design—Influence. I. Title.
NA712.H47 1983   720'.973   82–24983
ISBN 0–262–08127–X

CONTENTS

PREFACE

Some years ago, a well-known American art critic, claiming ignorance in matters of architecture, asked me why there were so many ugly new buildings around. He expected a convincing answer. In formulating a reply I realized that there appeared to exist a pattern of characteristics in most of the buildings cited in the course of our conversation, and that this pattern was related to the major constituents of the teaching ethos associated with Walter Gropius—that is, Gropius in his years at Harvard University (1937–1953) rather than during the earlier Bauhaus years.

The observations my friend and I exchanged were concerned not only with style but with the fragile and intricate yet tenacious connections between a teaching philosophy and its material manifestation, that is, between course content and teaching method and the appearance of a building designed by a graduate of a particular school. Obviously, the connection cannot be strictly causal, for too many unpredictable events occur between study and application. The student, in this view, is not like a cement truck going from loading station to building site, but rather like an ocean vessel that is sent to one destination but ends up at another, carrying much of its original cargo.

Walter Gropius is one of the founding fathers of modern architecture and, in a formal sense, its preeminent educator. Although many of us have assumed for years that Gropius and what he stands for, cloaked in the Bauhaus or Harvard mantle, are passé, the fact that many of the principal architectural practitioners in America today are graduates of his program at Harvard must be taken into consideration, or so it seems, if the question of the current condition of architecture is to be addressed. The word Bauhaus is, these days, used as a popular adjective, casting an aura of chaste elegance and benign efficiency on the object so described. But many more successful architects graduated from Gropius's program at Harvard than from the Bauhaus. Among those whose work is at the forefront of architectural practice today are Harvard Graduate School of Design alumni Edward Larrabee Barnes, John Johansen, Philip Johnson, I. M. Pei, Paul Rudolph, and Ulrich Franzen, to name only the best known. Also active until recently were the two most successful Bauhaus-trained architects, Marcel Breuer and Bertrand Goldberg. And there are two generations of younger architects in practice and a third in school, still being trained in programs that are offshoots of what was, during the war years and after, virtually the only progressive school of architecture in the United States. With all this in mind it appears apropos to stop for a moment and see what train we are on, architecturally speaking; here, I assume, modestly, the task of pulling some of the necessary brakes.

What may at first appear an American phenomenon with European roots turns out, upon closer inspection, to have worldwide implications. We all know it from history: when the United States became the most powerful of nations after World War II, it naturally became the object of the world's hopes in architecture and art as well as politics and economics. In Europe and Japan the American architectural scene was (and still is) watched very carefully for cues, deservedly or undeservedly. And since a model merits perhaps greater critical attention than its progeny, it is arguable that the buildings and teaching ideas discussed in this book are a valid target for criticism that seeks to uncover the sources of the disappointing state of architecture, since they played an important part in fabricating that model. Not only does a mutated version of the American model exert enormous influence within foreign cultures today but it is still being replicated with great vitality at home.

Once all this has been recognized, the subject matter assumes a certain timeliness, particularly in light of current debates among architects about the relative importance of values embodied in symbolism and rhetoric, structural expression, social consciousness, vernacular preservation and revival, investment return, or cost and energy consciousness.

At its most general, my subject matter concerns the fragility of the interrelationships between seeing and thinking, for maker and appreciator alike. Considering the confusion that characterizes thinking and production in architecture today, a confrontation with the most recently popular (some would add, still popular) architecture of past years might raise some overlooked questions, even if we can hardly hope that one essay will cause the digestion of a still very lumpy era.

I also have a pedagogical purpose, for the central issues I deal with pertain not only to the making and appreciation of all architecture but indicate by contrasting comparisons how certain fallacies can be avoided through a consciously critical attitude toward the past and the cultivation of a sensitive attitude toward its reinterpretation.

Rather than enter into a direct debate with adherents of one or another of the intellectual biases in the current architectural debate, I choose to present my critique as an internally coherent argument. The subject is approached directly, by analysis, explication, and criticism from the evidence or object at hand rather than by citing what someone else has said.

The principal method used to examine and explicate visual as well as verbal formulations is one of analysis and comparison, rarely used in architectural criticism. Phenomena are laid side by side rather than end to end so as to avoid implying a rigid cause and effect relationship. Thus the subject matter of the critique as a whole can remain open to further interpretation by the reader.

In order to make the subject matter and the examples cited accessible to anyone, only published quotations and examples of buildings have been used. For the same reason, as well as to strengthen a structural approach to the analysis, even at the expense of historiography, interviews were not conducted. The built work and the teaching intentions are meant to exist on their own merit.

And last, perhaps to be taken as a warning to unsuspecting readers, this essay is not to be understood as a minihistory of the Gropius and Breuer years at Harvard and the exploits of their former students. I think of it as an educated personal assessment of certain ideas and their manifestations.

Thanks are due Harriet Schoenholz Bee, Gabor Brogyanyi, Amy Anderson, and Frederick Shands for valuable editorial advice, and Geoffrey Siebens and Frances Campani for their essential work on the illustrations. The MIT Press provided valuable editorial and design assistance.

My special thanks to Colin Rowe who has unwittingly, in the course of many years, made it possible for me to doubt almost any architectural proposition, including the one illuminated in this book. And last thanks are due Clement Greenberg, whose conveniently naive inquiries about "all those ugly buildings" triggered the writing of this book.

THE DECORATED DIAGRAM

Today, more often than not, a building is an attention-seeking object that glorifies its owner and architect and is oblivious, if not outright injurious, to its physical, and often its social, context. Its plan is diagrammatic—a literal expression of functional relationships—and the nonshelter aspects of the exterior of the building appear to be reduced to one purpose: to excite the eye (in a purely physiological sense) by clever pattern designs or by a total absence of pattern. Visual cues incorporated in the design of the building defy intellectual and often emotional resolution because they appear to have no meaning beyond their own existence; they are simply recorded by the retina.

In short, the building becomes a haphazard record of such random events as program, legal restrictions or inducements, materials, plastic expression, building process, and icon quality rather than a manifestation of their considered coexistence, or better, their resolution into a coherent whole.

We can see similar phenomena in a well-known historical context, namely, that of the Bauhaus. In looking at published work by former students of Bauhaus-inspired teaching in Germany and America, we find many of the characteristics described, including the inducement of retinal excitement superimposed on a diagram and, most important, visual cues that lead nowhere—causing the suspicion that the Bauhaus/Harvard ethos is somehow related to the unsatisfactory state of architecture.

In exploring that idea, we are presented with a coincidence, namely, that ten or so of today's most prominent and successful American architects graduated from Harvard's Graduate School of Design (GSD) between 1942 and 1950. It was in those years that the school, by all accounts, represented most clearly the ideas of its prime mover, Walter Gropius, and his major collaborator, Marcel Breuer. Their tenures lasted from 1937 to 1953 and 1937 to 1946, respectively. While Gropius took charge of the program as a whole and taught the master's studio, Breuer taught the third year and final bachelor's studio. At first it may appear too pat to propose an educational link between the current condition of architecture and the so-called Bauhaus ethos, but there nevertheless emerges, upon close inspection, a pattern of characteristics that appears in many recent architectural works, and most prominently in those by Harvard GSD graduates of the forties and fifties.

The purpose of this book is not so much to prove a certain chain of cause and effect as to analyze and correlate the visual evidence and to demonstrate these relationships through what might be called the legitimacy of visual truths. Although there have been sporadic attacks on Bauhaus theory and teaching for having been too dogmatic (as represented by the expression "the Harvard box") or for having inhibited individuality, the criticism has rarely been made in terms of the formal characteristics of the school's teaching or products. I propose, therefore, to take a closer look at these characteristics, since it is through them that we derive meaning from what we see.

My stated undertaking is a possible if somewhat speculative explanation of the Bauhaus ethos, its implications, and its effects as emanated from Dessau and Cambridge. The all-encompassing motivation, however, is to demonstrate the need and a method for informed and deliberate control of form and space as an analog to all other aspects of architecture; to propose, for instance, that there be a certain spatial logic in a building that conveys to the viewer in narrative and associative terms the purpose and meaning of that building. What might be called palpable space (as opposed to conceptual space) is an important element in this transmission. I will return to these aspects of architecture in discussing formal structure.

But first a word should be said about my reasons for selecting the architects whose work I examine. Although rarely identified as a school or coherent group in this country, they have, nevertheless, collectively exerted considerable iconographic and moral influence on students, professionals, and potential clients from the moment their early houses achieved national acclaim through widespread publication in professional and household journals. The group includes Edward Larrabee Barnes, John Johansen, Philip Johnson, I. M. Pei, Pei partners Henry N. Cobb and Araldo Cossutta, Paul Rudolph, Ulrich Franzen, Victor Lundy, and TAC (The Architects Collaborative) partners John Harkness and Louis McMillen. Their student terms at Harvard are shown comparatively in fig. 1.

With their *Architectural Record* House of the Year and AIA awards these architects became bright young heroes to the students of the fifties and early sixties. To their professional colleagues they became legitimizers of the modern movement, for they knew how to domesticate the new, largely European demands on architecture as a social and political force. To prospective clients, who had read about them and their work in *House and Home* or *House and Garden,* they made contemporary architecture respectable. A client could bask in the rays of the avant-garde without risking a sunburn. Many earlier European patrons of modernism had not been so fortunate.

Perhaps more on the European than on the American side of the Atlantic, much was expected from this group, since they were the first crop of American architects to be given a Bauhaus training after the Bauhaus proper was forced to disband and Gropius accepted an invitation to begin again, under entirely new circumstances, at Harvard.[1] In postwar Europe, Gropius's Harvard students were regarded as unburdened or uncorrupted by centuries of history and years of war on their own soil and therefore as imbued with a quintessentially American mixture of optimism about the future and a sense of pragmatism in approaching it. Two publications in particular attest to the hopes for and early acclaim of their work. Barely out of school

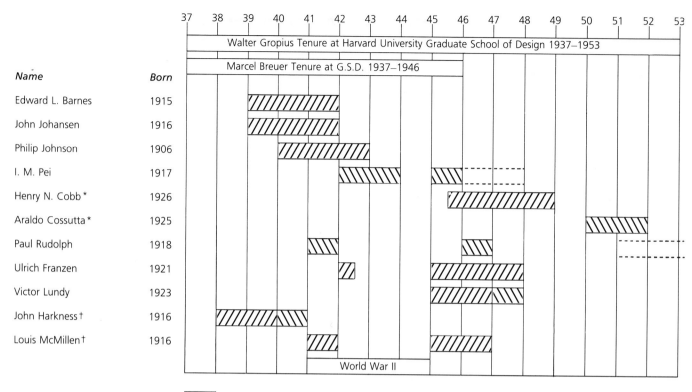

1
Student tenure of
principal architects in this
essay, Graduate School
of Design, Harvard
University, 1937–53.

in 1950, Edward Larrabee Barnes, Paul Rudolph, and I. M. Pei had their work published in a special issue of *Architecture d'Aujourd'hui* on Walter Gropius and his school, Rudolph serving as editor under Gropius's direction.[2] In 1957 Philip Johnson, John Johansen, Ulrich Franzen, Barnes, Rudolph, and Pei were among fifteen Harvard/Gropius-affiliated architects chosen, with twenty-five others, by the British *Architectural Review* for inclusion in a special issue (entitled "GENETRIX")[3] on the most important architects active in the United States. The numbers alone indicate the esteem in which the results of Gropius's years at Harvard were held at that time.

In order to put the impact of the early work of Harvard/Gropius graduates in perspective, it is important to remember that the terrain had been prepared for them for some time. The most emphatic and best organized among the propaganda instruments in the United States was probably the Museum of Modern Art in New York through its exhibitions and publications. MoMA's first architecture show, in 1932, and its now famous companion publication, *The International Style: Architecture Since 1922,* by Henry-Russell Hitchcock and Philip Johnson, aimed primarily at professionals and initiates among the public. Later efforts, however, such as the 1942 primer *What Is Modern Architecture?* were aimed at a larger audience, which had begun to flock to this cultural watering place. A peak of public success in the cause of legitimizing modern architecture (or, perhaps more correctly, its Harvard/Gropius mutation) was probably achieved with the 1949 exhibition of a suburban house designed by Marcel Breuer (figs. 4, 5, 6, 8). According to news reports, 70,000 visitors filed through the house, which sat, somewhat incongruously, in the museum's garden.

The question of the influence of the MoMA house and others like it will come up later in the essay. But first it should be useful to take a closer look at the house itself in order to pinpoint its characteristics. A comparison with a much earlier house by Le Corbusier suggests itself almost naturally because the latter also has a "butterfly" roof and is a residence of similar dimensions (approximately 23 by 72 feet covered by the main roof compared to approximately 27 by 68 feet for the Breuer house). This is the Errazuris house, of 1930, in Chile (figs. 2, 3, 7, 9, 10, 11). These houses, comparable in the ways just mentioned and in the use of rustic materials like flagstone and fieldstone, are utterly different in the attitudes they display toward architecture. While the first strains to accommodate an American middle-income family with the most efficient "zoning of functions" possible and then shower the resulting diagram with (by 1949) safely modern references, thus giving the occupants the feeling of living in harmony with the *Zeitgeist,* the second displays an intention not only of accommodating the occupants' immediate needs but of creating a basic confrontation between architecture as an abstract idea and architecture as craft and tradition.

The particular idea embodied in the Errazuris house is expressed in the realm of space and of visual cues for choice of action or mental association. The rationale for the disposition of areas of activity seems just as plausible as in the MoMA house, with the difference that in the MoMA house the zoning and its physical means—low fieldstone walls, louvered screens, flagstone areas and paths, and so on—pose as the architectural idea itself, while in reality they assume by form and disposition the importance of furniture, which is to say that they are no more than accessories to the architectural idea. This leads to a more literal interpretation of flexibility of use in the Breuer example, while flexibility is more implied in the Le Corbusier example since it is subordinated to a greater spatial and experiential concept. In the first house, the kitchen becomes the "control center" for a pragmatic reason—

2
Le Corbusier. Errazuris house, Chile, 1930, site plan, as originally conceived.

3
Errazuris house, section and floor plan as originally conceived.

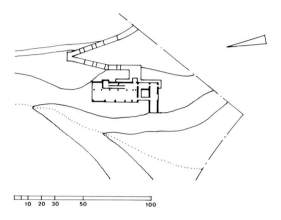

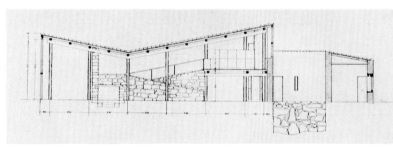

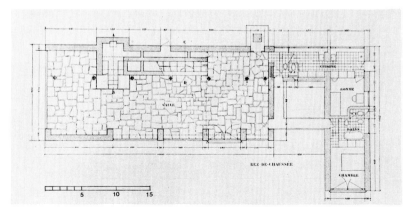

the lack of servants in their hypothetical middle-income family with several children. In the second, the kitchen is directly adjacent to but outside the house proper and *en suite* with the maid's room, leaving the main space in the house free for other uses.

Obviously there are two different life styles involved, one nurtured by the almost boundless optimism of postwar America, the other evidently more traditional in its context of middle-class Chile of the thirties. Notwithstanding the difference in social ambiance, there remains the question of the architect's idea, according to which he defines the space where any human activity takes place. These two architects, both part of the modern movement, believed their work capable of improving lives through improved living conditions. Hence, their most general intentions are, in fact, quite similar and are not to be disputed here. But in specifics their attitudes diverge, although they may bear superficial resemblances. Take, for example, the most obvious exterior similarity between the two houses—the butterfly roof (figs. 8, 9). How are its inherent spatial and symbolic qualities related to other important aspects of the house, such as site, orientation, entrance, internal organization of "programmed spaces," and methods and materials of construction?

In the Errazuris house, as is evident from the illustrations, the *V*-shaped roof interlocks with and thus enhances the meaning of several other aspects of the house, chiefly site and internal ramp. While the silhouette of the house recalls the far-off mountains in what might be called an abstract notation, the slopes of the ramp to the mezzanine inside coincide with the slopes of the roof and thus not only bind the two elements together formally but give a second level of meaning to the roof slopes.

By the further coincidence of the trough of the *V*-shaped roof with the line at which lower and upper legs of the ramp meet, ramp and roof are

4
Marcel Breuer. Exhibition
house, garden of The
Museum of Modern Art,
New York, 1949.

5
Exhibition house,
Museum of Modern Art,
section and plans.

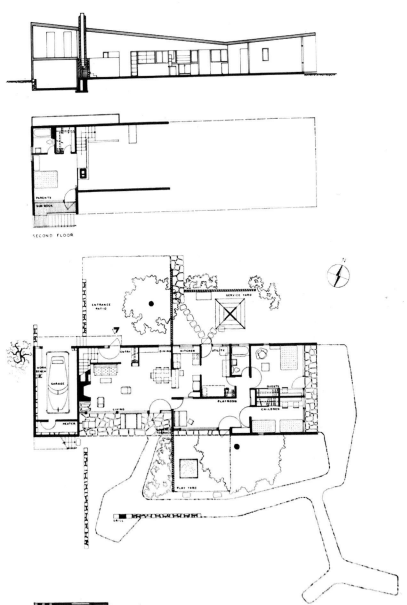

6
Exhibition house, view of
living room.

7
View from mezzanine of
a house by Antonin
Raymond, chosen by
Le Corbusier to illustrate
a comparable view in the
Errazuris house.

firmly positioned with respect to one another. This has the experiential consequence that, when ascending the ramp, at the midpoint landing one finds oneself momentarily in the most compressed spatial condition possible in this building but simultaneously looking through the most expansive window available: the entirely glazed north wall of the building, which, in the southern hemisphere, is the exposure that admits the most sunlight (fig. 7). The result is the experience of spatial compression and visual release beyond that is associated with walking through mountain passes.

As if this cue of replication between nature and artifice were not clear enough, the path down to the front door of the house is nothing but another, larger, more natural ramp—with only one switchback, like the indoor ramp (figs. 2, 7). Separating the two ramps is the front door into the main level of the house. Any door naturally marks a transition, in this case from vast outside to intimate inside. The problem for the designer is location and calibration. The two columns centered on the door just inside the entry appear to imply a vestibule, which is all that is needed here, given the location in the far south corner of the main volume and under the mezzanine, which, together with the massing of the ramp, also shields the entering visitor from the light and sun flooding through the north end.

Balancing the thrust of the roof is a most extraordinary feature of this small house: the deliberate nonalignment of the regularly spaced interior columns with the irregularly spaced piers along the west wall, through whose openings one sees the Pacific Ocean. It is questionable whether the interior supports are structurally necessary (the crossbeams could have been strengthened to span the entire 27 feet). They do, however, serve a visual function. The increasingly wider spacing of vertical elements implies an "accelerating" fan of sight lines between the round posts and their nearest opposite piers (fig. 11).

Reconciling the dominating north-south direction of the main volume with the almost equally dominating panoramic view of the Pacific. Thus the inherent spatial dynamics of the basic volume, which suggests a wide tunnel and therefore seems hard to penetrate at the two side surfaces, are "tamed" and even turned into an asset. At the entrance the visitor's eye is subtly coaxed along compartments of the ocean view, widening but in perspective brought closer, and is finally led beyond the north opening and the terrace *next* to the house and level with the floor inside. A far-off, breath-taking, scaleless, and unreachable experience has been transformed and brought back to an intimate and reachable one. What the mountain roof and exterior/interior ramp sequences have achieved vertically has here been achieved horizontally.

Subordinate elements of the three-dimensional composition clearly reinforce the major theme of the house, the conception of a veranda sympathetic to a difficult but dramatic site. First, because the maid's room and guest room are in principle detached from the main volume and because they form a small block of their own, thrusting forward of the house, it appears that the entire house supports the directional preference toward north (figs. 3, 9), despite the paradox that the larger of the butterfly "wings" points south. Without this assertion of preferred direction by "blocking" the house on its south end, and the additional employment of some subtler means to the same effect, the main volume would have a tendency to appear to be about to slide back and forth along the contours. Second in support of this directional shift is a horizontally striated railing, stitching its way north from the guest room across the little bridge and reappearing and ending in the second bay of the west facade of the main house. It thus emphasizes the first bay framing the entry. Moreover, it acts metaphorically as a tendon, as if to reinforce the unity of the house. That also seems

8
Exhibition house, Museum of Modern Art, view from patio.

9
Errazuris house, view from ocean.

10
Errazuris house, interior
view from entry.

11
Errazuris house, aspects
of formal structure.

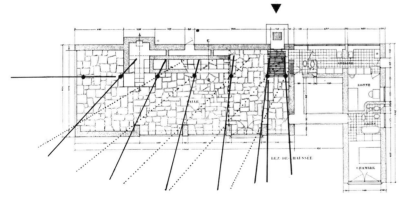

to be the principal effect of the third element, the maintenance of a strongly implied datum plane (at about 6 feet 9 inches above the floor), represented or marked by such disparate surfaces and lines as the soffits of the "panorama windows," guest room, and most other ground floor windows or doors, the lower surface of the spandrel beam supporting the upper windows at the north end, the top of the parapet to the midpoint landing of the ramp and, most directly, by the underside of the mezzanine at the lower level of the east-west crossbeams. This second, implied plane (the main floor being the first and real plane) not only ensures the reading of human scale, but, by creating a horizontal membrane, makes it possible to gauge and appreciate the extraordinary spatial configuration above it. In other words, the butterfly roof has become at once abstract and real by being locked into a coherent overall spatial and experiential structure.

Thus, in the Errazuris house, poetic allusions transcend not only function but space and mass and the means of their construction. In the Museum of Modern Art house, in contrast, it is difficult to detect any structuring of space other than the purely functional. There, because of a series of disconnected or misleading cues and an emphasis on physical elements as objects, the proverbial sum of parts appears to be, for once, less than the whole. For example, the valley of the roof, instead of being placed in a spatially and symbolically meaningful position—the valley, or underbelly, of a butterfly roof is surely its most distinctive feature—it happens to coincide with the wall between bathroom and utility room (fig. 5). Therefore, from inside the house one is aware only of a wedgelike space under which all public and a few private activities take place. Most important for the latter is the master bedroom, perched on top of the garage and beyond the fireplace assembly.

In the bulletin which the museum published on the occasion of the house's exhibition we are told that the double-story package of garage and "parents' apartment" is designed to be added at a later stage when there is functional need because of more children in the family or a desire for increased privacy.[4] Yet, however plausible this design decision may be from a diagrammatic and practical viewpoint, it becomes utterly implausible when the *form* of the volume of the house is considered. Surely one would expect an addition to be joined where the two roof slopes meet, rather than made into an arbitrary extension of one or the other of the butterfly wings.

This instance is not the only direct conflict of form with content. (Insofar as formal characteristics are *inherent* they are as much part of content as pragmatic considerations are.) A far more obvious discrepancy is that the western end of the funnellike space ends in a solid wall, in both the original and extended version. Indeed, the south facade roof and end wall are expressed as a continuous surface, as if the roof had been creased at its highest ridge and bent to become a supporting wall. The confusion of signals is complete with the evident detachment of the minor east wing from the dominant west wing by spatial noncommunication between the two, and by the deliberate expression of the east wing on the outside by vertical cypress siding that rises straight to the roof flashing and thus overlapping the exposed roof beam (fig. 4).

The hypothetical site being flat in all directions and the possibility of a play on mountains being improbable, the butterfly roof ("one of Breuer's better-known innovations," according to the description of this building in the major collection of his works)[5] makes less and less sense. Perhaps the possibility of tucking in an extra floor under a single sloping roof and the creation of "visual interest," as Gropius would call it, in otherwise dull surroundings are two intentions one might see realized. But do these motives—functional and decorative—justify the use of such an unusual roof shape? The roof, it seems, ought quite properly to be an essential part of the spatial idea of the house rather than a pretty trick.

In light of these questions about the plausibility of the roof it is not surprising to find a lot of talk about the "spaciousness" and "flexibility" of the MoMA house in the catalog. One is an emotive term, the other technical, but neither is descriptive of space or its manner of containment, let alone a spatial structure. This perhaps purposeful evasiveness certainly exacerbates the dichotomy between plan and appearance and becomes all the more poignant when compared to the Errazuris house, where, as it was described in 1935, "the rusticity of the materials is in no way a hindrance to the emergence of a lucid plan and a modern esthetic."[6]

To come to the point: although both houses employ rustic building materials and accessories, as observed earlier, the Le Corbusier house of 1930 subordinates them consciously to the greater idea of a "modern" spatial structure, while Breuer's house of 1949 accepts space, not as the originator or ultimate manifestation of all ideas touching on architecture, but merely as a semiconscious by-product of an essentially sentimental intention marketed as a level-headed scientific proposition (fig. 6).

The MoMA house exemplifies the functional zoning, expert attention to detail and craftsmanship, and endless play of textures, patterns, and materials (often as a substitute for spatial ideas, one suspects) that characterized not only most of Breuer's other houses but, more significantly, much of the architecture that some of his and Gropius's Harvard students were to build a few years later. Around the country, to deans, faculty, and students alike, the success of the Harvard/ Gropius graduates meant the consummation, if not consecration, of American Bauhaus teaching.

A survey of American architecture schools would almost certainly reveal that, even today, a great majority of them adhere consciously or unconsciously to a Bauhaus-inspired curriculum. The connection between the work of these Harvard/Gropius graduates and the teaching of architecture will be treated more fully in chapter 3. First, more should be said about the group's work.

While the major significance of grouping these architects lies in the collective and individual influence they have exerted on the professional and academic scene since the early fifties, minor importance might be attached to the similarity with which their careers progressed. With the exception of I. M. Pei and TAC members John Harkness and Louis McMillen, all began their building careers with suburban houses for the Eastern establishment in New England, New York, and Florida. (Pei was hired right out of Harvard by William Zeckendorf, the legendary urban developer and speculator of the fifties and sixties, to work on schemes in Denver and other cities). Again with the exception of Pei, their practices progressed at about an even pace from private-house clients to institutional clients who then commissioned schools, campus buildings and housing, theaters, and churches. Few examples of office buildings, other commercial structures, or public and speculative housing are to be found among their commissions of the fifties and sixties. Only beginning in the seventies in the wake of the urban renewal boom (or fiasco, depending on one's point of view) has their work become urban in locale and large in scale.

The predominant type among the works I examine is the single building (or self-contained building complex) on an open site—an ideal condition for expressing individuality as an artist-architect. For, curiously enough, all except the members of TAC rejected Gropius's exhortation to teamwork;[7] they set up offices run like ateliers with themselves as masters. Rationalist, European-bred anonymity for the sake of a cause was

not for them; they were, after all, enterprising and restless Americans, inheritors of the Protestant ethic and the Horatio Alger myth.

Among the general characteristics shared by many of the buildings produced by Gropius's illustrious students, it is relevant to note, first and as most important, that they are curiously passionless. Behind the camouflage of retinal excitement and frequently melodramatic gesture, few of the works show evidence of any struggle that might have gone into their designing, evidence that would betray an attempt to reconcile opposing functional and formal conditions or a struggle with a difficult site.

Furthermore, there appears very little evidence of a realization that, among many others, social and psychological problems ultimately have to find their resolution in aesthetics if the building is to be coherent. In other words, there is a tendency to separate the formal qualities of a building from its physical reality. This disunity is, present, as we will see, in many Bauhaus-legacy buildings. On the one hand the solution is meant to be purely pragmatic; on the other hand, it is intended "to create visual interest." Through wide publication and eager acceptance by the public, a kind of low-style tastemaking produced a climate in which other buildings of similar quaity and not necessarily by Harvard/Gropius graduates could prosper and thus further devalue what were the once rigorous standards of architecture. The architecture magazines of the fifties and sixties are full of examples.

The role of true believer demanded of the Harvard graduates, among many things, an almost reflex mistrust of architecture as art. And yet the Harvard group eventually converted to a belief in architecture as art; some professed this conversion explicitly in written manifestoes,[8] while others did so implicitly through their work. Perhaps the most dramatic and best-known declaration was staged by Philip Johnson, who said in 1949 to an audience of shocked Yale students, "I would rather sleep in the nave of Chartres Cathedral with the nearest john two blocks down the street than I would in a Harvard house with back-to-back bathrooms!"[9] Like many converts, they ran the risk of becoming zealots of the new religion, thus blinding themselves to its subtler points and the continuing necessity to question their assumptions in making decisions.

Oddly enough, some of their best-known early houses are by far the most spatially conscious buildings the members of this group produced. These early works are also among the least texturized and otherwise discordant in character. The admission of symmetry to the plan and facade gives some a neoclassic or even Miesian serenity which (except for some of Johnson's work) was not to reappear in later projects.[10] As a visual reference early houses by nine graduates of the Gropius-Breuer era are illustrated here (figs. 12–27). Almost every one was upon completion selected as Record House of the Year or received prestigious AIA and other awards too numerous to be mentioned here. The apparent difference in characteristics between early houses by these architects and the work of their teachers can perhaps be explained by avowed efforts to counteract the Breuer/Gropius influence when it came to "style"; Mies offered a purity of form which could match the purity of conscience expected at Harvard. An inability to sustain a meaningful counteraction in later and larger works will become clear as the discussion of these buildings progresses.

Having been educated in the Bauhaus ethos to be true believers (believers in such things as progress through technology and "returning to honesty of thought and feeling"),[11] the Harvard group seems to have assumed wit and other forms of humor in architecture to be immoral and frivolous. Humor did not square with the sense of mission and the dedication to truth and honesty required for the task of making "modern architecture . . . the inevitable consequential

product of the intellectual, social and technical conditions of our age,"[12] as Gropius proclaimed three years before he arrived at Harvard. Of course, architecture is not known as a medium of great comic capabilities. There are few buildings which are funny without being ludicrous. There is, however, one form of wit to which architecture is particularly susceptible, and that is irony, a didactic form of pretense, the art of expressing something by means of seemingly opposite meaning. Without it the architect is deprived of a useful and potent method for resolving seemingly unresolvable incongruities such as a conflict between form and space, site and program, or site access and building orientation.

An example of what is meant by irony in architecture is Le Corbusier's Besnos house in Vaucresson, near Paris, of 1922 (figs. 28–32). In this case, the glaring paradox of contrary formal implications is that the program is far too small in size and too modest in character for the site location, which is at the end of a surburban street joining, in a *T* shape, another road running past the lot. A second paradox, deriving from the first one, is that access by car straight toward the plot inevitably makes pedestrian entry difficult.

Le Corbusier's solution was twofold: he, so to speak, inflated a frog to the size of a bull and then had it squarely face the menace of being run over or walked past. Extruding the staircase in the plane with the street facade increased the facade surface by a third (fig. 28), while the gathering of garage doors, "Persian miniature" balcony, top windows, and roof reveal along the center axis of the same facade (minus stair) provided a powerful facelike assemblage (fig. 30). All subsequent design decisions regarding the street facade were made in concert with the first two.

These decisions have several consequences, most of them ironic. The largest entrance, and the hierarchically logical one, turns out to be the

12
Edward Larrabee Barnes.
Barnes house, Mt. Kisco,
New York. 1956 (Record
House, 1957), interior
view. From *Architectural
Review*, 1957.

13
Barnes house, plan. From
Architectural Record,
1957.

14
John Johansen. Warner
house, New Canaan,
Connecticut, 1957
(Record House, 1958),
view. From *Architectural
Record*, 1958.

15
Warner house, plan.
From *Architectural
Record*, 1958.

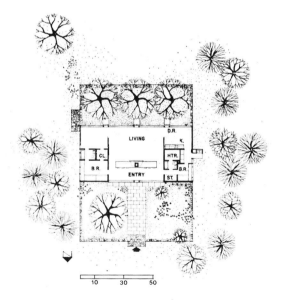

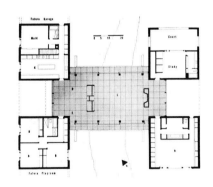

16
The Architects
Collaborative (Louis
McMillen, John Harkness,
et al.). Six Moon Hill
development, Lexington,
Massachusetts, 1948,
views of McMillen house
and Harkness house.

17
Six Moon Hill develop-
ment, site plan.

18
Philip Johnson. Johnson
house, New Canaan,
Connecticut, 1949
(numerous awards),
approach view.

19
Johnson house, site plan.

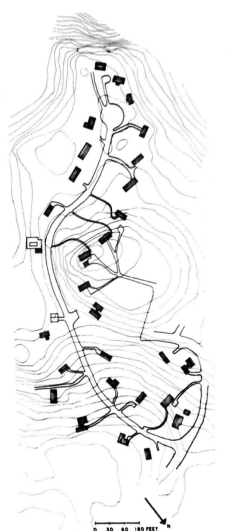

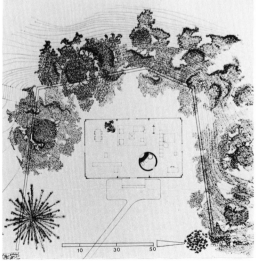

20
Paul Rudolph. Cocoon
house, Sarasota, Florida,
1950, view. From
Architectural Forum,
1951.

22
Ulrich Franzen. Beattie
house, Great Neck, New
York, 1957 (Record
House, 1958), view. From
Architectural Record,
1958.

21
Cocoon house, plan.
From *Architectural
Forum*, 1951.

23
Beattie house, plan. From
Architectural Record,
1958.

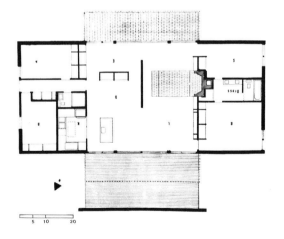

24
I. M. Pei (with Henry N. Cobb and Araldo A. Cossutta). Apartment helix project, 1949, cutaway model view. *From Architectural Forum*, 1950.

25
Apartment helix project, floor plans. From *Architectural Forum*, 1950.

26
Victor Lundy. Herron house, Sarasota, Florida, 1957 (Record House, 1958), view. From *Architectural Record*, 1958.

27
Herron house, plan. From *Architectural Record*, 1958.

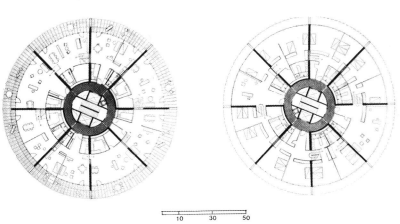

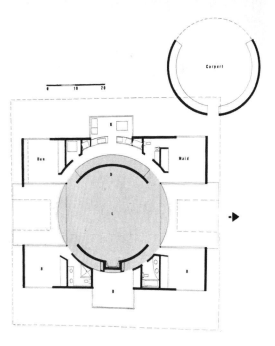

28
Le Corbusier. Besnos
house, Vaucresson,
France, 1922, view from
street.

29
Besnos house, staircase.

garage door; yet, being on axis with the oncoming street, it clearly welcomes cars more readily than pedestrians (fig. 32). That gives rise to the polemical question, with all its attendant interpretations, of which is the real entrance: garage door toward the center or pedestrian door to the left leading to the attached stair? The latter door, visually pointed to by three spatial events—marquee/balcony, recessed staircase windows, and a sieve of inset portholes—is evidently vying for attention with the garage door assemblage, which is more extensive but subtler, making, in the end, man versus car a philosophical issue through the means of architecture.

All this posturing on the front facade makes it actually too large and apparently massive compared to the few rooms inside, its outside having little correspondence with what lies behind it in total opposition to the modern movement belief that the exterior of a building should reflect its interior, or that "the plan should generate the facade," as Le Corbusier was fond of saying. In fact, the facade, in trying to intervene between public and private space, is made to act as a screen, reinforced by the transverse interior circulation just behind it (fig. 29). To announce the use of irony, the thin vertical slab of the staircase is expressed and visible when one approaches the building from one side, lest one expect a real *palais* behind that large wall (fig. 28).

If we accept, for argument's sake, the phrase "false front" to describe the essential characteristic of Le Corbusier's house at Vaucresson, then we are likely to be reminded of pictures of Main Street in the typical nineteenth-century American town, (fig. 33), which became the Main Street of pioneer America. We might also recall two recent apartment house facades designed by two Harvard/Gropius graduates and built along New York City's Main Street, Fifth Avenue. One, by Ulrich Franzen, is at 800 Fifth Avenue (figs. 35, 36, 39), just north of the southeast ("Plaza")

30
Besnos house, elevation

31
Besnos house, plans.

32
Besnos house,
reconstructed view from
street leading toward
house.

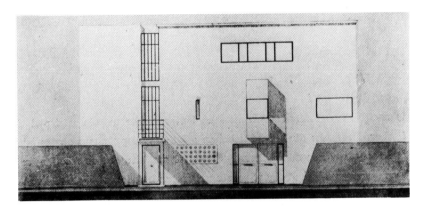

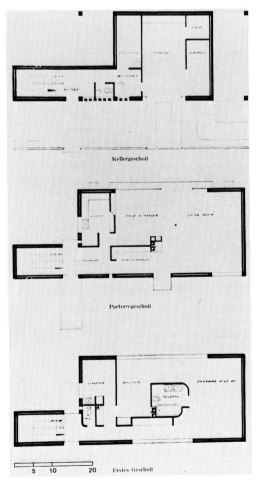

33
First Avenue, Corry,
Pennsylvania, about
1868.

corner of Central Park; the other, by Philip Johnson, at 1001 Fifth Avenue (figs. 37, 38, 40),[13] rises directly across from the Metropolitan Museum of Art. Both form part of the wall of buildings that faces Central Park (fig. 34).

At first glance, because both the old and the new examples are characterized by false fronts, they appear to have used irony to reconcile conflicting conditions. At least on a superficial level this is probably true of all of them, but only knowingly employed as a design tactic in the two apartment houses.

On traditional Main Street the false front was imbued with meaning beyond its own existence. Main Street represented *urbanity,* symbolically assuring inhabitants and visitors of the presence of civilization as they knew or imagined it to be. In order for the daily rituals of town and city life (and therefore a civilized identity) to be preserved in frontier conditions it was necessary first to *perceive* a town, or at least its main street: substantial-looking facades with lots of windows forming the two walls of a street, with porches running along them.

Unfortunately, the population and resources of a pioneer town often could not provide the scale and substance needed to sustain such an impression of urbanity. Thus false fronts served to reconcile conflicting aspirations and realities. They concealed gabled, barnlike construction, which was the cheapest and fastest to put up but would have looked too uneven along the street, perhaps like a quaint village but certainly not like a "modern" town, fit for pioneers. A horizontal, if broken, roof line on both sides of the street made for a much stronger (more palpable) definition of space than a succession of uneven gables would have, giving Main Street, often also used as Town Square, the desired "urban look."[14] Although irony was the unnamed result of an instinctual response to conflicting desires and realities, and not the product of calculation based on a deliberate esthetic theory, the false fronts of the pioneer towns' Main Street appear equally necessary and successful in reconciling incongruous conditions.

In a similar way the two Fifth Avenue false fronts are backed by conflicting considerations: easy and economical construction of the actual building versus elaborate and expensive construction of the facade. In the latter cases for certain but perhaps also on Main Street, a speculator-builder, after producing the raw bulk and the interior layout of the buildings, turned the facades over to architects, with the obvious intention of lending glamour to otherwise undistinguished buildings. Yet here, the ironic devices, although most likely intended to help resolve the contextual problems of scale and style, appear part of a capricious play with the building's neighbors and the street wall. The exaggerated scale of both buildings is partly due to the great number of apartment units that were, for economic reasons, to be piled on each site. To make things worse, view being naturally at a premium, the facade surface tended to extend to its allowable maximum in order for more apartments to overlook Central Park. Along that part of the park's eastern border, the turn-of-the-century mansions are about six stories, the apartment houses of the 1920s to the 1950s are fifteen, and some built since are about twenty stories. The Franzen building at 800 Fifth Avenue (1978) rises to thirty-four stories, and 1001 Fifth Avenue (1979) by Johnson to twenty-two stories, the latter extending another three stories in the form of a blank wall.

In respect to the more literal aims of this essay, it is interesting to note that both Johnson and Franzen were actually given the task of decorating a diagram, which effectively became their program. Although not particularly famous buildings, 1001 and 800 Fifth Avenue merit discussion because they are in essence ordinary developer

34
Fifth Avenue, along Central Park, New York, about 1975.

35
Ulrich Franzen. 800 Fifth
Avenue, New York, 1978,
facade in context. From
Process Architecture,
1979.

36
Ulrich Franzen. 800 Fifth
Avenue, New York, 1978,
proposed facade. From
Process Architecture,
1979.

apartment buildings, typical in program and site, and because they represent a practice increasingly popular with developers, that of hiring a prestige architect to design their facades and letting him worry about context, scale, and stylistic issues. The dichotomy between plan and appearance that results in a decorated diagram has thus been institutionalized. It seems particularly ironic that Harvard/Gropius graduates, presumably reared on Total Architecture, have executed two of the more prominent commissions of that kind.

If at Vaucresson, and somewhat less on Main Street, the problem was how to inflate a frog to bull size, then here the opposite problem presented itself: how to make a giraffe look like a pony, or, at least, a horse. While Franzen, at 800 Fifth Avenue, tried to pretend that there is no giraffe by hiding it behind the apparition of a pony resembling its neighbors on either side, Johnson, equally wishing the giraffe away, gave it the features of the next-door pony. In other words, both buildings play out a rather literal heavy-handed charade, almost as if the purpose of the game were to prove that irony or wit in architecture is not possible.

Although, looking at the Beaux-Arts mansion turning the corner next to 1001 Fifth Avenue, one recognizes the reiteration of the bay windows, the base rustication, and the reference to the mansard roof in Johnson's building, as well as the weltlike facade divisions referring to its other neighbor, the borrowed elements seem to exist disconnectedly. Instead of means that would visually tend to reduce the towering height of the building and prevent its present threatening posture vis-à-vis the Metropolitan Museum of Art, the four files of bas-relief-like bay windows, accentuated by a stark material and color contrast of dark glass and metal against off-white stone, run up the facade like so many zippers. The effect is exaggeration of an already very tall facade by use of vertical in preference to horizontal accentuation. Another consequence is the near-destruction of the facade surface, which is sliced into alternating strips of glass and granite.

The contrast between those elements on the facade which respect context, and thus would support cultural continuity, and those which defy it appears so literal, even violent, it leaves one wondering at what, or whom, such impudent rhetoric is aimed: The weighty seriousness of purpose exuded by the museum across the street? The neighboring traditional buildings of the establishment? The developer-client? Perhaps it is the presumably wealthy tenants of 1001 Fifth Avenue itself, who might interpret architectural impudence as personal flattery.

Put another way, the formal elements and maneuvers appear to be an amalgam of an entire list of contradictory formal and symbolic qualities: solid versus fractured; real versus ephemeral; unique versus contextual; magnified smallness versus obvious largeness; luxurious versus cheap; serious versus sham; mature versus decadent. Each of these self-negating pairs of attributes naturally is analogous to a pair of specific formal characteristics. To explore them all in detail here seems redundant in the presence of illustrations and in the light of what has already been said.

There is one area of the building's exterior, however, which, because its formal and symbolic characteristics are in large measure responsible for the attributes listed, merits explication. This is the top of the facade. In elevation it appears as an uninterrupted expanse of flat surface, continuing the vertically extended planes of the lower facade, uniformly covered in granite. Its height is about three stories, but from the street appears indeterminate for lack of comparative human scale and because the expression of floor intervals tends to be suppressed by the zipper effect of the evenly colored succession of glazing and spandrels (figs. 37, 38). While in projected

37
Philip Johnson. 1001 Fifth Avenue facade, New York, 1979, view to the south.

38
Philip Johnson. 1001 Fifth Avenue facade, New York, 1979.

39
Ulrich Franzen and Philip
Birnbaum. 800 Fifth
Avenue, New York, 1978,
plans (typical floor and
ground floor). From
Process Architecture,
1979.

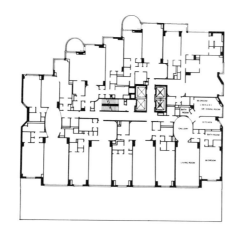

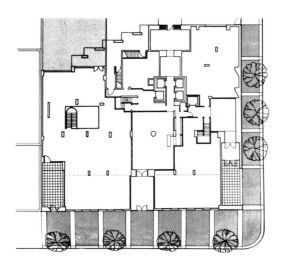

outline it alludes to the mansard roof of its little
neighbor, it looks, in fact, more like an Egyptian
pylon on account of its shape and material.

What thus stands as the epitome of weighti-
ness is visually supported only by insubstantial-
looking strips of glass and granite veneer, made
to interlock by the application of a granite mold-
ing delineating the shape of a battlement. Looking obliquely at the facade, the natural view
when walking down the avenue, the mansard-
roof-cum-pylon apparition suddenly becomes a
billboard, ostentatiously held upright by gigantic
struts, revealing the "architect's" facade as a thin
plane disassociated from the "speculator's"
building behind it.

Not only have references—as literal as they
may be—to the respected and presumably
trusted past switched instantaneously to associations with present-day pop culture and even
punk but, by that mental transition, supported
by the formal coincidence of bottom of "fore-
head" surface with baseline of "pylon," the top
portion of the facade has been almost totally
severed from the rest. It is as if the rigid battle-
ment-shaped moldings had become a piano
hinge, around which the mansard roof/pylon/bill-
board would flap forward should imaginary mag-
nets be released at the upper end of the struts.

The question presents itself whether this display of unnerving effects amounts to a deliberate
use of irony for the purpose of reconciling conflicting conditions, or whether, because of self-
contradictory design actions, essential order and
control have been lost. In the absence of such
formal concepts as fragment *versus* whole and
multiple interpretation of a given form or composition, so knowledgeably demonstrated in the
house at Vaucresson and, more naively, on Main
Street, the apparent intention of 1001 Fifth Avenue appears to dissolve into an array of unrelated and therefore confusing anecdotes. It
seems self-evident that only through the use of
structured formal allusions can two or more read-

ings exist simultaneously, precisely because those readings are merely suggested and are made complete only in the beholder's mind.

In contrast to 1001 Fifth Avenue, the facade of 800 Fifth Avenue by Franzen appears rather as a nonfacade: physically emaciated because it is only one among four sides of an essentially freestanding tower and is formally neutralized by the application of a tartan weave of glass, spandrels, and wall, precluding any hierarchical reading usually associated with entry facades. The top of the building, instead of being a cheap-thrill eyecatcher like 1001 Fifth Avenue, lacks articulation entirely. The center line down the front is further obscured by making the eye vacillate between the nearest narrow and wide bands of openings as forming the central zone of the facade.

The modesty, if not matter-of-factness, of the pattern adorning the Fifth Avenue facade, while being quite in keeping with the obvious intent of diminishing the "shout" of this towering newcomer to the Fifth Avenue "wall," causes an unintended irony at the expense of the building.

Here an independent building with separate functions (commercial, medical, and others) and facade (spacing, proportioning of openings, materials, and so on) is set in front of the residential tower as a kind of camouflage. Besides the particular disposition of openings, the camouflage intent is most strongly expressed by making five floors appear as three (as was, surely to Gropius's chagrin, often done in the facades of classical architecture). To pay tribute to context, most of the building's formal cues were taken from its northerly Georgian-style neighbor and a few from the low-lying corner portion of its southerly neighbor, the stripped-down Beaux-Arts Hotel Pierre. To be sure, borrowing from neighboring buildings is in itself a time-honored architectural device. By spreading its wings, as it were, 800 Fifth Avenue inevitably increases in importance, as befits a public building of corresponding func-

40
Philip Johnson and Philip Birnbaum. 1001 Fifth Avenue, New York, 1979, plans (typical floor and ground floor).

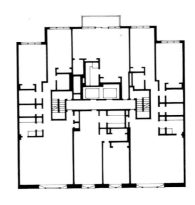

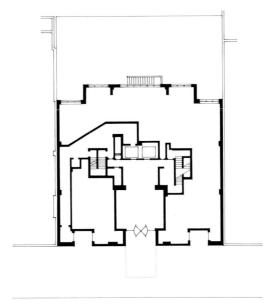

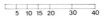

tional/symbolic importance, perhaps a church, a transportation terminal, a seat of government, or even a hotel. But here, paradoxically, *extra* attention is being drawn to a tower which, by its private function and evenly patterned appearance, has been rendered most reluctant to fulfill the role of paramount object which the ("detached") false facade and its extensions set it up to be.

From the more distant point of view of the critic, the glaring contradiction between intentions and means, emphasized rather than resolved by the use of irony in the false-front street facade, appears symptomatic of the central flaw in the Bauhaus legacy: a weak connection between eye and mind and its corollary, attributing to an *intention* the qualities of an architectural *idea*. While both buildings, 1001 and 800 Fifth Avenue, potentially represent a combination of entrepreneur and architect that is fascinating from an economic standpoint, it seems most beneficial to user and onlooker alike to search for a subtler interlacing of interests and solutions than the principle of "divide and rule" can offer.

Formal structure is what makes analogies and metaphors possible. And without conscious thinking and seeing in analogies architecture becomes dry and mechanistic and essentially unproductive in its most exalted task, namely, to offer the beholder an intellectual challenge and an emotional reward whatever its pragmatic duty.

In much of Gropius/Harvard–influenced architecture, it is the lack of control over apparent analogies, intended or unintended, which makes one doubt whether the formal characteristics of a given building (as representable in drawing form) were ever recognized, much less employed to ends beyond the diagram and some retinal stimulation. Between lofty and often worthy ideals of social improvement and their physical expression there appears to be a large zone of poorly informed formal decisions or even a failure to recognize that decisions had to be made at the level of form/use analogs which reach beyond programmatic function.

The term *formal structure* is meant to define the underlying order and its effects on any natural or man-made object or phenomenon—from a thunderstorm to a tree, from a song to a building—based on inherent formal properties such as symmetry (axiality), hierarchy (progression), climax, repetition, and others, to which, singly or in combination, may be ascribed analogous functional and symbolic attributes and values. While formal properties are fixed through time and varying cultural conditions, values are not. A particular formal structure may be judged good or bad, important or unimportant, depending on prevailing cultural circumstances and the beholder's intentions. In other words, the term formal structure couples definitive formal givens with their latent interpretations and transformations realized through human instinct, imagination, knowledge, and ingenuity, which, in turn, are often governed by tradition, time, and place. However, no interpretation or value judgment is possible without first *recognizing,* that is, seeing, inherent formal properties and their interplay and effect on each other.

Francis Bacon, the sixteenth-century English philosopher, compared the shapes of tables and their effects in promoting or inhibiting a certain kind of discourse:

A long Table, and a square Table, or seats about the walls, seem Things of Forme, but are Things of Substance; for at a long Table, a few at the upper end, in effect, sway all the Businesse; but in the other Forme, there is more use of the Counsellours Opinions, that sit lower.[15]

The perceived meaning of a long rectangular versus a square table depends upon a particular hierarchical political/social symbolism, that of a leader sitting at the short end of the long table, projecting or receiving, as it were, the predominant axis, the other short end usually remaining open. Sitting on one of the four equal sides of a square table, however, the leader is obviously in a much weaker hierarchical position and open to greater, perhaps more representative influence from his council. The myth of King Arthur and his knights has become inseparable from the idea of a round table, symbolizing in literary terms what is implicit in formal terms; that a circular table is as likely to promote good will among its users as an oblong table is to promote adversity. The president of the United States sits neither at the short end of the long cabinet table nor randomly along its sides but in the middle of one long side, flanked by his most important cabinet members. He thus visibly occupies the position of a chief, but, as signified by the wideness of the table and the even spacing of seats around it, is also "one of the team."

In recent history, the most graphic and politically important instance of deliberately manipulating the shape and symbolism of a table occurred in the 1968 to 1969 peace negotiations between the United States and South Vietnam on one side, and North Vietnam and the Vietcong on the other (figs. 41, 42). North Vietnam was intent on establishing the equal status of the Vietcong even at the price of doing the same for South Vietnam, while South Vietnam vehemently opposed giving the Vietcong any legitimacy, even at the price of merging its identity with the United States, so long as the two pairs of allies were clearly distinct from each other. Hence, North Vietnam and the Vietcong proposed a square table and the United States and South Vietnam a long rectangular one. Evidently each side was aware of the inherent formal properties and correlative political meaning of each shape and rejected the opponent's proposal for precisely that reason. In their second proposal North Vietnam and the Vietcong were willing to talk around a circular table, thereby figuratively elim-

inating the identity of all participants. The Americans and South Vietnam still insisted on recognition of each pair of adversaries and therefore proposed, after many variations were rejected out of hand, two semicircles with a neutral zone between. This was also rejected by the North Vietnamese and the Vietcong because it still did not express the equal status of the Vietcong either by articulation (square) or submersion (circle). After weeks of further haggling a compromise was designed: a solid circle with two secretarial tables opposite each other across the round table. Finally it got to be a matter of inches. Eighteen magical inches separating the circular table from its rectangular satellites brought the agreement to sit down.

What is clear in this example is that the parties never disagreed about the meaning of a given form, and that both recognized and cherished the political symbolism implied in form. The circle with its rectangular satellites eighteen inches removed was apparently the exact configuration which accommodated the North Vietnamese/Vietcong intention of interpreting the circle as unbroken. At the same time the United States and South Vietnamese could claim, because of the rectangular tables' alignment and closeness to the round table, that there really existed two distinct areas divided by a middle zone marked by the side tables. In short, a dual interpretation was made possible by deliberately creating a multivalent form, allowing the coexistence of two fundamentally opposed political positions.

A table being the field on or across which untold human transactions take place—from a writer's solitary ruminations to portentous political meetings—its shape, its intrinsic geometric properties, are crucial to its effective use, and thus it is a classic example of formal structure "at work." The principles governing the formal structure of a table, expanded to encompass the space or room in which the table is placed, the relationships among spaces in a building, and the

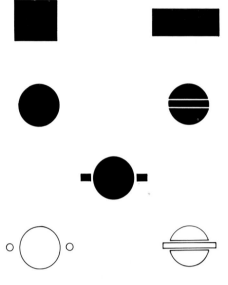

41
Analysis of table shapes proposed for Vietnam peace conference.

42
Table shapes proposed for Vietnam peace conference. From the *New York Times*, January 17, 1969.

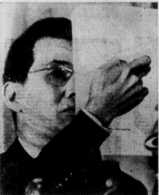

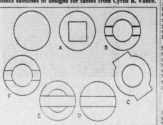

setting of the building itself will be applied in critiques in the following chapter.

A particularly rich and complex yet eminently "readable" example of this process can be gleaned from a brief look at the dining room in Villa Mairea by Alvar Aalto, built in 1938–1939 in the woods of western Finland (figs. 43–49). The intention of explicating this particular space is to demonstrate the possibilities for multivalence without loss of clarity within one room and, by inference, the operation of this quality in architecture as a whole.

The most singular feature of the Villa Mairea is the placement of the dining room within the disposition of all the architectural elements (figs. 48, 49). What appears at first to be an inexplicably ambivalent location—partly in and partly out of the building—for this one-story boxlike room, slowly giving way to a higher, more agitated entrance hall, becomes on close examination more plausible, if not actually necessary in terms of the dining room's special meaning in this house.

In many cultures, and especially in climates where winter darkness and summer daylight make the days and nights almost indistinguishable, as in Finland, shared meals often assume ritualistic aspects, be they seasonal, religious, national, or familial. Eating together provides a kind of family clock, particularly if the family is large and its members are independent, as here, so that the dining table and room around it quite naturally become a source of stability in the life of the household. Thus we find that the Mareia dining room is the only rectangular, closeable space within the honorific part of the ground floor and, furthermore, the most strategically located in respect to all parts of the compound (fig. 49). It takes on a new character if seen in terms of a general planning grid; even one with hierarchically dominant zones is in keeping with designing the dining room primarily as a box (figs. 46, 47).

Viewed from outside the building but inside the courtyard, the dining room, clearly appears as a quasi-independent object inserted into the larger of the two arms of the *L* shape of the main mass. The notion of insertion is encouraged by the illusionistic effect of seeing the dining room mass reflected in the living room window (fig. 44). Meanwhile, the notion of object—connoting singularity or special purpose—is suggested by an elaborate orchestration of mutually reinforcing architectural events—formal, functional, and symbolic. These aspects serve to amplify the governing theme of the building: the development from nature to artifice. In fact, the dining room, as seen from outside, can be interpreted as a vehicle for the crossover from one end of the spectrum to the other, from sauna (nature) to living room with studio (artifice) above or vice versa.

There are several evident formal structural contributions to the suggestion of the dining room as object and central thematic vehicle. The first of these is the white stucco framing the window on three sides, the fourth side, turning the corner toward the loggia, being of ultramarine faience tile. The second is the exterior flagstone fireplace with steps cut into the deck directly above the dining room; and the third is the wood deck itself, surrounded by a vernacular wood railing—obviously being played off against the steel-pipe railings on the roof which, by 1938, had become a hallmark of the modern movement. Also, while dividing the honorific and utilitarian domains of the ground floor, the dining room is placed within the area of public activity but at the same time is systematically related to the service block. More precisely, the service block is centered on the dining room and, as drawn in published plans, the dining table itself (fig. 48).

However clearly determined the dining room's position vis-à-vis the service block might be, its dimensions are less obviously determined. One or the other of two imaginary transformations

43
Alvar Aalto. Villa Mairea,
Noormarkku, Finland,
1936, foyer and entry to
dining room.

aiming to conform to a strict *L* shape within the four-by-four regulating grid might at least explain its larger dimension (fig. 47). Either the dining room and its immediate vestibule would be aligned with a two-module zone of the regulating grid corresponding to the living room area, or the dining room—entry hall—canopy complex would be pulled back into a four-module zone. In either case, the exercise would make clear an intermediate, coherent zone between service and living areas within which the dining room attains its own domain. Functionally, like the typical domestic dining room, it must relate to both sides, although for different reasons. The shift out of register only emphasizes the importance of all the elements, one following the other, from canopy to Janus-like fireplace.

Within the dining room there appear to be two privileged positions around the long table. The supreme position, the farthest from the entry, corresponds to the head of the table, while the nearest to the entry, opposite the head of the table, corresponds to the next most important position. The other seats are distributed more neutrally along the sides of the table. Traditionally, the father would occupy the head, like a reigning monarch or chairman of the board, and the mother (official contradictor, or more likely, director of the service coming through a door near her) would occupy the opposite side.

There are, however, two important spatial and symbolic characteristics which are peculiar to the father's position. He is the only one to see straight along the axis of the table and the room through a series of receding planes (fig. 45). The last plane is also the first through which one enters the house by means of an external but enclosed vestibule, in axial alignment with the table and dining room. Furthermore, a band of clerestory windows above the house entrance allows him to see the pine woods in front of the house, and perhaps even the other side of the little valley. This unique axial view is augmented

44
Villa Mairea, view from pool.

45
Villa Mairea, dining room.

46
Villa Mairea, aspects of
formal structure.

47
Villa Mairea, aspects of
formal structure.

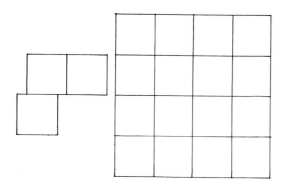

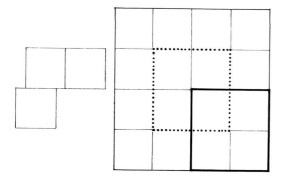

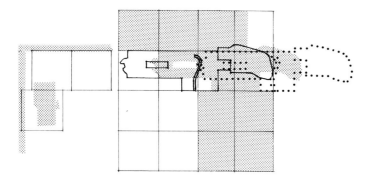

by a diagonal view to the right, piercing the entire living room. Depending on the time of day, the glass of the living room might even reflect the pool and the forest beyond, thus adding yet another degree of richness to this supreme position which symbolically distinguishes the head of a household.

In contradistinction, the mother, looking straight ahead along the entry–dining axis, can contemplate her husband silhouetted against the dining room's asymmetrical fireplace, while through the window she can see the sauna, the pool, the garden court, and the pine forest— things natural or traditional. Most of these views the father would only see reflected in an artifice: the living room windows.

The pair of formal/symbolic analogs represented by the difference between the father's and the mother's perceptions of the dining room and, beyond it, the house as a whole, appears to be philosophically and socially rooted in the traditions of the bourgeois family. There exists another pair of analogs, related to the first by the sharing of space, territory, and longitudinal axis, which in and of themselves are rooted in a philosophy of universally applicable formal/symbolic analogs. If the former pair represents a highly specific value structure, the latter does not. It concerns the entry to the house.

The visitor is received gently by a deep canopy and led through a vestibule box into the main foyer, which, in keeping with the entry's uniqueness and symbolic importance, is the only space in the building to express one module of the four-by-four grid of approximately 22-foot-by-22-foot units that guides all major functional and spatial boundaries. A foyer typically contains architectural announcements about the surrounding building, if for no other reason than that of orientation. This purpose, taken literally, is served by the apparently freestanding curved wall. Its primary purpose is to lead you toward a few steps

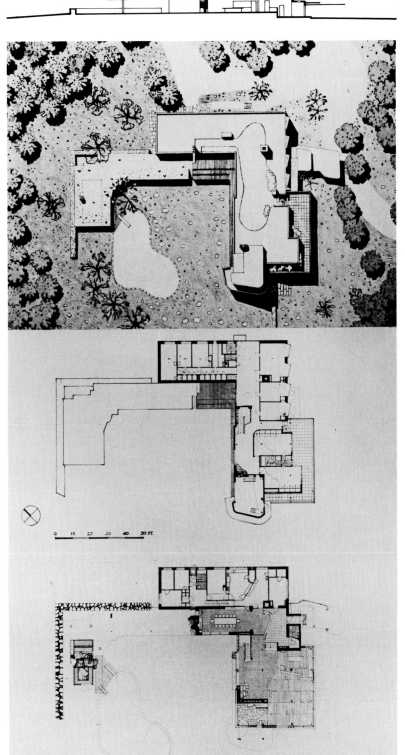

48
Villa Mairea, section and
plans.

49
Villa Mairea, axonometric
view: disposition of
dining room.

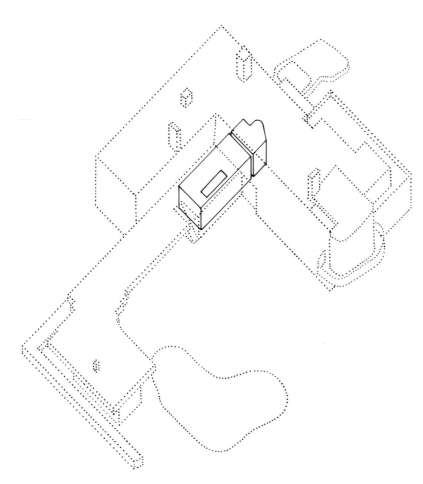

to the living room. Since the dining room, though straight ahead, is not visible from the entry portion of the foyer, one's eye and attention are caught by the bulge (about six feet in height) that meets the visitor. But, looking back from the living room, it is apparent that the wall also forms the physical and visual dividing line between lower and upper foyer, the latter serving the dining room in the same way in which the foyer serves the house (fig. 43). This figure-ground conjunction of purposes, together with the axial alignment of vestibule and dining room, further underscores the importance accorded the Villa Mairea dining room.

As if to indicate the dining room's allegiance to the other living spaces, the same terra-cotta flooring is laid "around the corner" into the principal living room. A narrow by-pass circulation band along the service block can be interpreted to serve the same ends. The band begins by preventing the curved wall from touching the service block with a small set of steps and, after doing the same to the dining room fireplace, it is stopped by a suitably shaped pier some distance removed along the rear of the loggia.

It is by the very nature of the task difficult to describe simultaneous architectural events and their significance in any building. This is particularly so in the case of Villa Mairea and perhaps in Aalto's architecture in general. In Villa Mairea's case this difficulty is probably exacerbated by a deliberate refusal to form a spatial ensemble of discrete elements and a corresponding insistence on exploiting the formal notion of multivalency. Besides the location of the dining room itself, consider its immediate foyer; its parapet is at once retaining wall and object, appearing as a freestanding wall which separates, yet also unites, the upper and lower level. One is not quite sure whether the informality of spatial dispositions within the foyer area encourages a similarly informal use or allows a more formal use, if one responds to the boxlike boundaries of the enveloping space and the latent axiality, and perhaps interprets the bulge in the wall as a balcony. Most likely either is possible once the plausibility of one or the other interpretation has taken root in one's mind, as determined by one's mood and intentions, natural or artificial lighting, and strategically deployed props. Stepping back a bit from this close-range analysis, it may aid a clearer understanding of the formal principle of *cue* and its interpretation to remember that the principle relies on instinct and that it can operate on all levels (figs. 50, 51).

Although Villa Mairea may at first appear difficult to decipher, in the end all important decisions are seen to have their justification and to be linked in alternate series, each with its own set of analogies. In sum, the building reveals itself to be but a means by which to construct one's own world instead of being an end in itself, a decorated diagram.

50
Girl in Venice, 1958: response to a manmade condition, a niche between two church pilasters.

51
Holi festival in India, 1965. Response to a natural condition, the shade of a palm tree.

In this chapter I will examine in detail some representative Bauhaus-legacy buildings in terms of the characteristics I have proposed—dichotomy between plan and appearance and, on the part of the architects, a certain blindness to formal structure and a general reluctance, if not inability, to experiment with new solutions when the occasion invites inventiveness on a fundamental level.

The first example is Philip Johnson's Sheldon Memorial Art Gallery in Lincoln, Nebraska, of 1963, a good illustration of a seeming rejection of the Bauhaus ethos for the sake of artistic license (figs. 54–57, 61). Here the architect's propensity toward the sort of classical grandeur traditionally associated with institutional or personal power, although antithetical to Bauhaus ideas, is quite apparent. But, true to Bauhaus teaching, the architectural methods by which the effects of architecture as art and the experience of grandeur are achieved are just as literal and mechanical as the ones employed in designing the much-denounced Harvard box.

It should help clarify these statements to compare the Sheldon Art Gallery to a building which might have served as its model, Karl Friedrich Schinkel's Altes Museum in Berlin, completed in 1830 (figs. 52, 53, 58–61). It is a hypothetical rather than a historically certifiable precedent, but it serves as a contrasting solution to the same program type.[16] It is obvious from a cursory look at the two buildings—or, more precisely, their published pictures and plans—that they have in common some basic elements of formal structure. Despite their differences in size and proportion (about 150 by 100 by 35 feet for Sheldon and about 296 by 184 by 64 feet for the Altes Museum), as well as period and culture, both are characterized by a freestanding, oblong, rectangular container, divided, parallel to its short sides, into three zones. The middle zone dominates by its central location and by its unique formal and functional significance. Furthermore, on the major approach sides of both museums, the unity of the facade is represented by the use of uniform, rhythmic vertical divisions.

Perhaps the more glaring difference between the two is the relationship of facade to plan and the disposition of spaces inside the building. The Sheldon Art Gallery is essentially composed of two decorated boxes pulled apart to leave a void of the same dimensions; the Altes Museum is complex and finely orchestrated to multiple themes, gathered into a hierarchic whole. While schematically the uniform rhythm of vertical elements along the main facade refers to the unity of the building in each case, the means used and the path of refinement chosen produce facades at opposing ends of the scale of visual and intellectual interest.

The facade unity achieved in the Schinkel museum derives from the expression of the vertical elements as a freestanding colonnade set into a tight frame provided by end walls, base, and roof (fig. 52). Termination of the facade by walls instead of columns and the use of the classical device of narrowing the end spacing allow the colonnade to be perceived as an entity, like seeing the forest before the trees. Moreover, a row of columns set in front of a wall always constitutes a figure-ground relationship. While the columns play the more readily apparent part of figures, the spaces between them can be equally effective figures. Schinkel's portico behaves as the laws of perception would have it, except that in addition it displays a more subtle application of the figure-ground phenomenon. The colonnade as a whole, by virtue of its uniformity, offers a ground against which the recessed wall/colonnade ensemble becomes the figure. The result might be described as multiwave visual and spatial oscillations, from small to large scale, from solid to void, from front to back, and from extremities to center.

Finally, the play of sun and shadows breathes life into this already formidable spectacle. The facade, owing to this controlled use of a natural element, is not only an aesthetic tour de force for the intellect; it speaks directly to the emotions. The sense of time, always present when moving around and through a building, here acts in a different and complementary manner. While the viewer stands still, the building may alter its appearance by the minute and through the seasons. On every encounter there will be new nuances, new moods, new occasions for interpretation.

For instance, you may be subjected to the struggle for attention between two simultaneous formal/symbolic aspects of Schinkel's colonnade. One is its appearance as an independent screen that seems to move past incidental architectural events, tending to generalize the building behind it by ignoring all hierarchic elements. Symbolically the colonnade and, by association, the whole building tend to be seen as anonymous and therefore free to be mentally appropriated and interpreted by anybody, at any point in time, like an aqueduct. In its other interpretation, the screen of columns can be seen as integral to the building, firmly locked in place, and therefore serving as the outermost transition from the strictly articulated interior spaces to the universal exterior space, suggesting a classical temple. Together these two interpretations vastly expand the scale of visual/spatial oscillations mentioned earlier, to the point where the method of shifting attention promises to become the governing idea of the whole building, facade and plan (fig. 53). This principle, it should be pointed out, is more than visual effect: it is a means of engaging the viewer's intellect and emotions in active discovery and enjoyment of the Altes Museum.

The main facade of Johnson's Sheldon Art Gallery, by contrast, presents a scheme that seems to nullify all human passion, not to say engage-

52
Karl Friedrich Schinkel.
Altes Museum, Berlin,
1822, entry facade.

53
Altes Museum, plan.

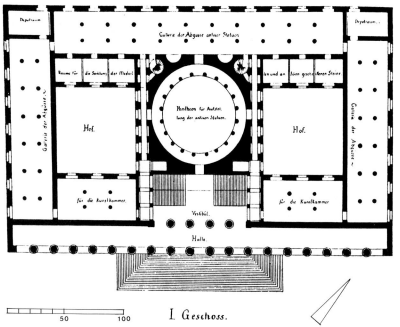

ment. The calculated orchestration of physical, spatial, and temporal elements and forces into a vibrant yet serene whole in the Schinkel facade is reduced in Johnson's museum to a single chord straining to evoke a sound of grandeur. Although finely crafted travertine—evoking grandeur—covers the entire facade, the shaping contradicts traditional associations with institutions. What might be meant to recall a colonnade or portico is actually a travertine skin pulled over a concrete frame. Looking like the webbing of duck's feet, it induces some visual, quasi-physical tension along the sloped and curved surfaces which form the boundaries of each cartouche-shaped panel. Where, in the Altes Museum, there is spatial and temporal tension, even oscillation, in a facade of framed identity, we find here a nearly two-dimensional pattern, stretched across the major facade and eventually—if one walks around and into the building—enveloping both exhibition boxes and the building as whole.

There is some plausibility in responding to an open site, which is surrounded by casually dispersed groves of trees so typical of college campuses and lacks strong spatial cues (fig. 56), with a building of continuous facades, particularly if it is to be entered on two opposing sides. It is just as plausible to find Schinkel responding to his site (fig. 60), which he himself chose and shaped and which has strong spatial and symbolic cues—consisting of the "tree wall" to the east, the castle front to the south, and the edge of the canal to the west of the huge square—with a building which has one dominant facade defining the northern limit of the square, while the other three facades resemble each other. The intentions in each case may be equally valid; it is their respective development which makes the difference. While the first chooses to stay within the range of surface manipulations, the second explores the powers of spatial events to realize its intentions. Where one facade freezes into decoration, the other opens up countless opportunities for human participation.

In the Sheldon Art Gallery facade we can observe that on account of a slight reveal which sets off the continuous skeleton, the walls seem to slip behind the quasi-pilasters to form a conceptually continuous plane which, in turn, defines the two closed volumes as boxes. This suggests a strongbox whose content is at once to be treasured and kept hidden. This unwelcoming imagery, which seems to be a paradox in a public museum, is reinforced by the choice of a catwalklike stair/bridge combination which looks weightless yet threatens to collapse on you in its fall to its original state of flatness should you find yourself under the double-cantilevered upper landing (fig. 55). Oddly enough, owing to its frontal symmetry and hinged diagonals, you may also have the uncomfortable feeling that you are about to be devoured by some enormous insect. Such sensations of uncertainty behind the seemingly almost impregnable facade, with its comparatively tiny entry through a vast glass membrane, add up to either a calculated frustration test or the result of an object-fixated, style-drunk design process or both. Such sensations are anything but the subtly calibrated interplay of architectonic elements and ensembles in the service of human comfort and the heightening of self-esteem which we can find in the facade and entry sequence of the Altes Museum.

There is one attempt in the Sheldon Art Gallery entry space to articulate a distinct hall or lobby in what would otherwise be the gap space trapped between the two gallery masses. The ameliorative attempt consists of giving the pilasters a double role (fig. 55). First, having the same shape and spacing (except for those added to hold the glass membrane) they reinforce the definition of each box as separate, thus keeping the original diagrammatic reading of the space as the consequence of positioning the two masses. Sec-

54
Philip Johnson. Sheldon Memorial Art Gallery, University of Nebraska, Lincoln, 1963, west facade.

55
Sheldon Memorial Art Gallery, view of entry hall and staircase from east.

56
Sheldon Memorial Art
Gallery, site plan.

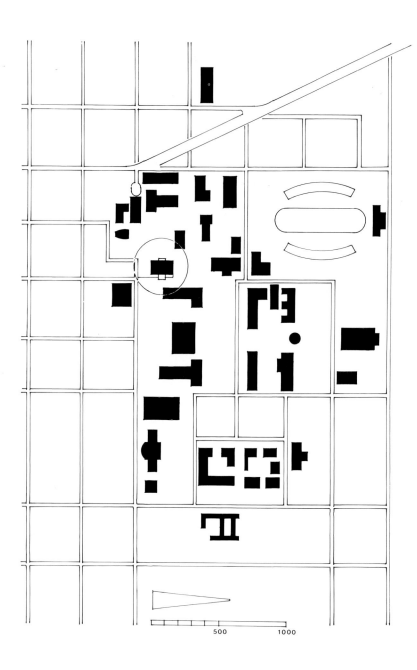

500   1000

ond, by extending the pilasters into the vaguely coffered ceiling with the same formal idiom, and by arranging for visual appropriation of the two pilaster-shaped columns at each open end, a certain amount of identity and stability is gained.

However, on account of the configuration and alien construction materials of the stair, excepting the tread treatment, one is never quite sure whether the opposing walls or masses are (figuratively speaking) about to be pushed farther apart by the pair of stair runs or moored in place by the bridge. It appears, therefore, that whatever stability of the entrance hall is gained through one means is lost by another, adding to the feeling of uncertainty called forth by the stair assembly alone. The entire play of sensual agitation in the hall and on the exterior of the building, quite in contrast to that of the Altes Museum, does not resolve itself in a deeper understanding of architecture, but, instead, alienates the viewer by reducing evolving action to two tableaux: view of building set in gentle park and dramatic-looking stair ensemble set in bellows-like space with grove of trees in the distance.

Within the entry, the stairs appear to consume all the space around them, to such an extent that they become the principal object exhibited in this museum, demoting bona fide sculpture in the same space to the status of decorations or humble bystanders at a grand event. It ought to be mentioned that the stair alone is not to be blamed for this condescending treatment of the sculptures; again, the visual agitation caused by the prismatic pilasters cutting into the hall space like wedges contributes its share. The stair's very quality as object, aided by its monumental scale, deepens the dichotomy between the programmatic raison d'être of this building, the art galleries, and its perceived raison d'être, the stairs.

While these stairs may be visually unique, their chief function is to convey visitors to the galleries. Hence, the more pronounced the dichotomy the more necessary it seems to introduce transition elements, for instance, neutral spaces of appropriate size and proportions, in order to guarantee a perceptually and emotionally coherent entrance sequence for the visitor. Instead, the hierarchically structured approach to the galleries, leading the visitor to expect a correspondingly significant formal, functional, and emotional culmination, is cut off with guillotine sharpness as he or she steps into either set of galleries from the bridge.

Consistent with the image of the hermetically sealed box, the layouts of the galleries, one being arbitrarily different from the other, do not recognize the privileged condition of entry from the stair since they have symmetrically disposed and similar openings, in the form of windows, overlooking the entrance hall. By being arranged *en filade* laterally across the gallery level the two windows and two doorways serve to suggest a certain unity for the building as a whole; yet, lacking support of the same kind elsewhere—for instance, all gallery doorways could be related in a consistent manner—the *en filade* idea remains as isolated from other ideas as the galleries are isolated from the stairs.

In contradistinction to Johnson's Sheldon Art Gallery, the single most inventive element in the formal structure of Schinkel's Altes Museum is precisely its vestibule-stair ensemble, inventive because it resolves demands made on various levels of consideration with great economy and elegance of spatial and functional arrangement (figs. 52, 53, 58). Besides literally giving access to the galleries and the rotunda on the lower and upper levels, the vestibule, including the stairs, forms the most important conceptual and experiential element of transition between the open square and the closed galleries. It is clear that Schinkel saw a visitor's entry sequence neither as a purely technical problem of circulation nor as an isolated "exciting" event, nor simply as a by-product of other decisions. He must have recognized the need for slowing down the visi-

57
Sheldon Memorial Art Gallery, section and plans.

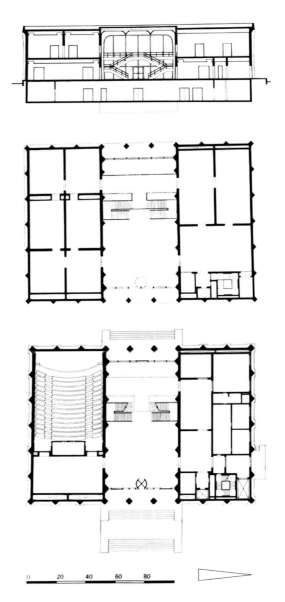

58
Altes Museum, Berlin,
section.

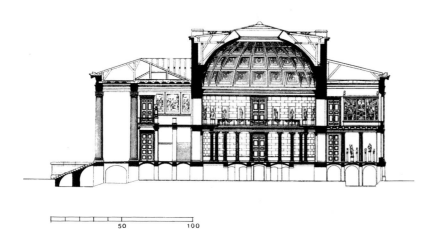

50   100

tor's pace, both physically and mentally, in order to remove him gradually from everyday routine and make it possible to enter a mood of contemplation appropriate to the appreciation of art.

The genius of Schinkel's solution seems to lie in the fact that it allows everybody his own rate of transition—we are reminded of the individually adjustable interpretations of the facade—by designing vestibule and stairs as much for direct movement as for lingering. Obviously, transition has to be as effective toward and into the galleries as out of them and back into the city, with different architectural features appearing prominently, first in one direction and then the other. On the way in, for example, the pediment-shaped stair wall simultaneously announces movement straight ahead, upward, and to either side. On the way out, however, the inner and outer rows of identical columns, silhouetted against the bright, open square, are naturally most prominent. Their gigantic scale, in relation to the size of the vestibule space and the observer, who can see them only from a short distance, lets the partially revealed city appear at a scale comparable to that of the paintings and some of the sculptures just seen, thus providing an essential psychological continuity in which there is time to pause (fig. 59). The visitor may want to reflect on what he has just seen or prepare for the mundane things which await, by strolling about the balcony or the lower vestibule. He or she may be aware of, but also feel protected from, the world beyond. Architecture, somehow, seems to be most effective when it makes possible such moments of suspension between one's inner and outer world.

In further explicating the entry sequence, one could see the two diagonal edges of the stair wall as abstract boundary lines of an incomplete triangle rising to its implied apex, reinforcing the axial location of the portal and thus offering a strong cue for actual entry. Should the condition be reversed, however, the same abstract inclined lines might represent ascending stairs, and the portal could be seen, when closed, as an abstract rectangle or wall decoration, or, when open, as a neutral void almost keeping the two stairs from meeting.

Therefore, when entering the vestibule with the intention of going to the painting galleries on the upper level, one is confronted with two almost equally strong but somewhat mysterious cues of how to proceed forward and upward; mysterious not only because of the latent formal-functional reversals but also because the lower halves of the flights of stairs are neither exposed nor intimated to the entering visitor (fig. 61). Mystery, implying conflicting signals and pretense, seems to have been employed here to a good purpose, the reconciliation of two conflicting concepts, just as Le Corbusier employed mystery's cousin, irony, to resolve a conflict between a small, private program and a publicly prominent site.

As one is led to expect in approaching the building, the configuration and spatial character of the stairs themselves play a crucial part in tying the building together conceptually and experientially, outside to inside, facade to plan, lower to upper level, utilitarian to honorific spaces, and uncontrolled exterior light to controlled interior light. On the way in, the visitor climbs the front steps, passes through the outer colonnade across a shallow layer of space and through the inner colonnade into the vestibule. This last space, on eye level, also appears to be shallow, tending to force movement straight through it toward the opening under the stairs or to either side into the sculpture galleries.

Two spatial events take place between inner colonnade and stair wall, as if to urge one by spatial means to decide how to proceed. One space is sensible as the eye moves upward toward the balcony and the ceiling, in the course

59
Altes Museum, upper vestibule.

60
Altes Museum, site plan.

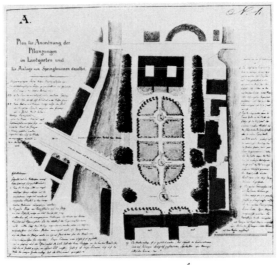

61
Altes Museum and
Sheldon Memorial Art
Gallery, axonometric
views; aspects of formal
structure.

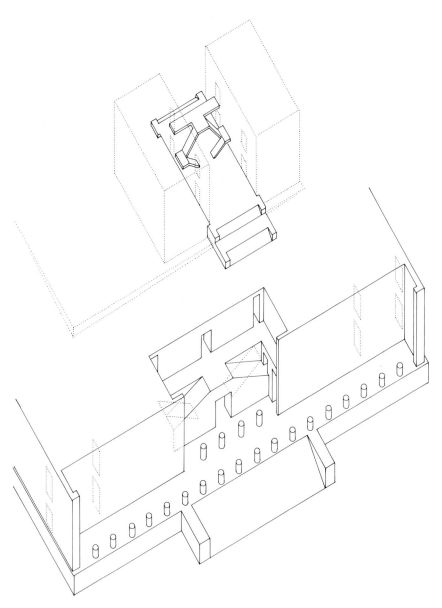

of which the shallow space perceived at the lower level of the vestibule is gradually transformed by a succession of recesses into a volume three times the depth and height of the same space at eye level. The beams on the ceiling run perpendicular to the facade and obey its divisions, thereby continuing its vertical rhythm in a slower tempo. They thus not only bind the greater vestibule plan to the facade but subordinate the functionally more literal, perhaps more human-scale lower vestibule to the spatially more complex greater vestibule, which is itself more in scale with the building as a whole.

The other, simultaneous spatial event is caused by the alignment of the doorways *en filade* with the narrow dimension of the lower vestibule (figs. 53, 58). The turn toward the galleries is made less abrupt by this means, since the vestibule can be interpreted as being at once part of the galleries to the immediate right and left and by implication part of the ring of all galleries, which, needless to say, reinforces a smooth transition from outdoors to indoors and from forward to lateral movement. On the conceptual level—perhaps to be consciously experienced after careful observation—the same *en filade* arrangement of doorways, identical on both floors, with their implied, corridorlike space locked into the first pair of windows on the east and west walls, accomplishes a number of other things which help to organize and animate the building.

First, it tends to free the wall behind the colonnade, not to the degree of independence and identity of the colonnade, as observed in the discussion of the facade, but commensurately less, for the outer surface of the wall is perceptually and in terms of its honorific purpose associated with the colonnade in front of it, while the inner surface serves the pragmatic function of a wall in any art gallery. In contrast, we are reminded of the diagrammatic treatment, devoid of any spatial idea, of the same general condition in the Sheldon Art Gallery. Second, and as a corollary to the first accomplishment, the inner block of spaces—stairs, rotunda, courtyards, and small galleries—is similarly detached and unified, with the help of two opposing pairs of doorways and windows looking into the courts on the northern side of the building. Again we see how on this level of the museum's formal structure the abstract values associated with geometric conditions match corresponding functional and symbolic meanings.

Formally, the vestibule and the two flanking galleries are neither completely contained within the two north-south galleries, nor totally attached to the facade ensemble, nor strictly autonomous. They become to a greater or lesser extent any one of a combination of these conditions, depending on the functional and symbolic meaning required of them by program and siting or expectations encouraged in the visitor by a progression of visual cues. Therefore, design and effect of facade and plan, as we now see, share the design principle of multivalency, just as facade and plan of the Sheldon Art Gallery are governed by the principle of a "univalent" diagram, decorated where visible to the eye. Applying the same principle to the interior and exterior of a building, however, does not guarantee automatic affinity between the two. It is ultimately through the act of formal/symbolic interpretation that the two aspects interrelate. Hence the greater the number of parallel interpretations possible, the richer the building and its experience.

The stairs in the Altes Museum, as we observed earlier, are crucial to the unity of the building. They appear at once as the principle object in the vestibule and a minor erosion of the building mass. Their scale seems colossal in respect to the vestibule but appropriate to the collection of spaces they lead to. The fact that they also appear to be carved from a large mass, rather than set into their own space—as in the Sheldon Art Gallery—mutes their object quality to the point

where it is difficult to know whether one is climbing or descending an independent flight of stairs or moving effortlessly on a continuous surface such as a ramp.

The visual ambiguity between object and relief, noticeable even from across the square outside, is confirmed and heightened by physical involvement when one uses the stairs (fig. 61). A spiral climb beginning under the balcony and upper runs of the stairs leads up through the tunnel-like first run to an intermediate landing, from which one continues up to the open second run to arrive on the balcony landing, overlooking the point where the journey began. By this ingenious means the entering visitor literally experiences the stairs as being, first, integral with the mass of the building and, second, an object occupying the middle of the vestibule space. The contrast between the two sequential experiences may perhaps be felt as analogous to the experience of the mystery and momentary disorientation below and the gaining of clarity, overview, and dominance above. One gradually becomes the other through vibrating upward movement at a constant rate, except for a pause for rest and reflection on the intermediate landing, almost as if some kind of cleansing process were intended, preparing the visitor for his encounter with man's most perfect state, which lies in art. Mozart's *Magic Flute* may come to mind in a musical analogy.

The stairs are also, with respect to a higher level of the building's formal structure, the most finely scaled manifestation of a three-part sequence of conceptual relationships, based on the little-known but effective design principle of prefiguration and recall, in the relationship of the landings to the stair, the stair and balcony to the vestibule, and, finally, the vestibule to the building. Because of this progression of similar relationships, the visitor is able to relate himself to the museum by visual and mental translation at all scales.

A discussion of the rotunda space has so far been deferred for the reasons that it is, despite its hierarchically dominant location in the plan, hidden from the visitor and because it has no corollary in Johnson's museum. The rotunda is announced on the outside of the building but is visible only from some distance across the square, and even then the dome is camouflaged by a low-lying rectangular box. It submits itself to the mass of the building and its main facade, also marking the position and lateral extent of the vestibule and thereby serving as the backdrop for the stair in a scenographic interpretation. Looking at elevation, plan, and section together (figs. 52, 53, 58) we find the rotunda embedded in a clearly articulated mass of cubic proportions whose uppermost region is identical with the roof protrusion visible on the exterior. While the rotunda space is unique in form and position with respect to the other spaces, as perceived from within (perception of position relies on remembering the position of entries in respect to adjacent spaces) from the outside its mantle conforms to the prevailing rectilinear geometry, thus neutralizing, if not denying, its presence. Because it is the focus of the entire facade composition and more in scale with the "backdrop" wall to the stairs and the vestibule, the large portal presents itself as the only clue which leads one to expect a commensurately large space beyond it. But because that expectation is put momentarily in question by finding that it also gives access to the stairs, the rotunda space, upon piercing the mantle, still comes as a great surprise. While on the plan the axis of the entry sequence continues through a door on the opposite side, perceptually the domed space appears as the goal of the sequence on account of an emphasis on the centrality of the space by the even spacing of the columns and the abstracted, almost hovering circles made by the balcony.

More often than not the middle zone of a tripartite, diagrammatic plan is developed functionally and symbolically to recognize and serve the building as a whole. The result is frequently, as we well know, one central dominating space symbolizing, among other things, arrival and announcement of the general purpose of the building, and actually organizing major circulation routes and means, as well as many ancillary functions. The Sheldon Art Gallery represents one of these schemes. The Altes Museum, however, divides the traditional single space into two successive spaces: the first (vestibule) accommodates the most important program functions and a narrow range of symbolism, mostly associated with entering and leaving the building, and the second space (rotunda) assumes such symbolic meaning that, formally, it almost becomes a separate building. On a higher level of consideration, this assignment of the two chief attributes of a traditional entry sequence to two separate spaces may be in itself seen as a symbolic expression of a preference for a "working museum," whose rationality brings it and the artworks it contains closer to the visitor, over a "show museum," whose primary purpose would be to impress upon the visitor the aspirations to power and glory of those who commissioned or designed the museum, thereby alienating the viewer from the art if not the building. By concentrating symbolism of rest and permanence in the form of the rotunda, the actual galleries are left free to respond more directly to the needs of display. No matter how the viewer's emotions might be aroused by looking at paintings and sculptures, he will always find calm and reassurance in the eye of the storm: the rotunda. The metaphor of a storm may be brought to mind, in formal structural terms, by the sequential arrangement along the building's periphery of long spaces of the same cross section and horizontal axes—implying *horizontal* movement of body and eyes, impelled forward by the depth of perspective—in contrast to the unique domical space in the center of the building, suggesting a pronounced vertical axis, implying rest of the body or measured movement along the rotunda's perimeter and *vertical* movement of the eyes.

Because of the rotunda's location, central although relatively isolated from the rest of the museum, visitors are not compelled to acknowledge the space and all its implications at a predetermined point; rather, they are allowed to ignore it or choose to incorporate it into their visit according to individual purpose and mood. Again, as in the facade-entry sequence, we find in Schinkel's Altes Museum that quality of noncoercion, coupled with clearly defined opportunities for choice on a conceptual and pragmatic level, which can only be conducive to every visitor's personal enrichment.

In trying to understand the formal structure of a building, it is often useful to generate a hypothetical transformation from the building's most elementary, unyielding, and abstract diagram to the final multivalent, resilient, and accommodating reality. Along the way one might find some formal explanation for those aspects which are otherwise not readily understandable.

For example, when looking at Schinkel's and Johnson's plans side by side, with the intention of distinguishing collections of spaces which, together, appear as coherent figures (roughly in the sense of "gestalt") governed by bilateral or quadrilateral symmetry, we can see in both plans a shift of figures with respect to one another along the axis of entry. Presumably these shifts, or planimetric agitations, respond to some real condition, whether it be site, program, or symbolism, given or self-imposed. In the Altes Museum we find two dominant, interlocking figures, together encompassing the whole building. One consists of the portico, echoed by the service spaces of the same width in the rear of the building and completed by the two side galleries and courtyards. In and of itself this figure clearly distinguishes between front and back of the building, stakes out its four corners, and implies its

center. The other figure is composed of the central rotunda, holding front galleries-and-vestibules and rear gallery together. Its center, and therefore the rotunda's, is shifted to the rear by the depth of the lower vestibule, another distinction of the dominant front from the anonymous rear of the building.

The most obvious of many effects of the noncongruency of rotunda and building centers is the muting of the hierarchic importance of the rotunda in symbolic and functional terms, which effect is then strengthened by various means of camouflage, as discussed earlier. The point here is that the abstract effect of the plan order is the generator of subsequent design decisions which ultimately result in the real effect, or the plan is the real effect's imprint, depending on synthetic or analytic intentions.

In Johnson's plan we can distinguish three figures, one shifted in respect to the others, and instead of interlocking they are overlapping. The stair figure hovers above the figure of the entrance hall, confirming the importance of the main entrance by its plastic form and slight displacement to the "rear" of the building. The congruence of quadrilateral symmetry between the figure of the entrance hall and the total building block reinforces the unyielding unity of the museum, as observed earlier in the discussion of the facade. What is lacking in conceptual resiliency in the entrance hall is made up for by retinal agitation: decoration of the undifferentiated ribbing of walls and ceilings and huge perforated gold medallions buttoned to the ceiling. In this swish environment the stair itself can hardly be expected to represent more than a caricature of a museum stair such as the one in the Altes Museum.

The third figure, represented by the podium from which hall and stair rise, does not do much to enrich one's possibilities of interpretation although there are a few steps added to the main entrance side, and the two gallery masses seem to encroach a bit on it (fig. 61). The three figures being within the same zone, being literal and hence easy to grasp, they become self-contained objects—podium, hall space, and stair—rather than formal analogs to spatial, functional, and symbolic events.

In conclusion, we have in the Sheldon Art Gallery a clear example of an unmitigated dichotomy between plan and appearance. The democratically homogenized interior spaces will always come as an inexplicable surprise after the authoritarian prelude of the exterior and the central hall. Their clash makes a mockery of both concepts. As in so many other buildings belonging to the Bauhaus legacy, space is not used as a primary organizational and experiential medium. If space had been thought of in such terms, the clash of conceptual with perceptual aspects of the Sheldon Memorial Art Gallery might instead have become an interesting discourse between two contrary forces of contemporary significance—democratic homogeneity and authoritarian hierarchy—and thus enriched the experience for every visitor by manifesting that struggle and inviting him or her to participate in it emotionally and intellectually.

It appears from this and other examples that design objectives in Bauhaus-legacy buildings have often been reduced to two criteria: derivation from a functional plan and creation of visual interest. These are viewed as independent criteria, each doing its job, resulting in a lack of dialogue or mutual reinforcement between plan and appearance. This deficiency becomes even more serious if we take plan and exterior appearance to be analogs of such fundamental architectural dialogues as inside–outside, invisible–visible, and conceptual–perceptual, all of which take place in the medium of space, which is consciously articulated for the purpose of explaining, mediating, ordering, and enriching this cluster of dualities. And here we get to the cen-

tral deficiency of the architecture under discussion: there is little sensation of space as a medium under the control of the architect and having distinct or positive figural characteristics. Space tends to be equated in these works with air or area; in other words, it tends to be residual in nature, as opposed to its use in the Aalto and Schinkel examples.

Let us pursue this theme further. On the one hand, space is conceived by many Bauhaus-legacy architects as the universal, all-pervasive medium displaced by solid objects (buildings and rooms), much as a rock displaces water. And, on the other hand, they are likely to think of space as an area between objects and walls that is adequate for the conveyance of people and goods or for activities such as those appropriate to a living room, corridor, theater, or factory. While the first concept is a passive acceptance of space as so much air between solid objects, the second gives it purely functional significance; it becomes a convenient bookkeeping way to translate a building's anticipated uses and activities into a physical container by calculating the necessary areas in plan and section.

An elementary example should illustrate what I mean: the project for a library and administration building for the School of Law, Economics, and Business Administration of the University of Tunis, designed by The Architects Collaborative (TAC) in 1961 (figs. 62–64). We might begin with the supposedly apparent observation that a square is a square is a square, whatever else it might become once the inauguration ribbon is cut. The refusal to recognize the inherent characteristics of this geometric figure, which obviously governs the form of the building—four symmetrical sides strongly implying a central vertical axis—accounts for the lack of correspondence between the organization of interior spaces, circulation spaces in particular, and the basic geometry of the building. If the program-

62
The Architects Collab-
orative. School of Law,
Economics, and Business
Administration, University
of Tunis, Tunisia, project,
1961, east elevation.

63
School of Law, University
of Tunis, project, plan.

64
School of Law, University
of Tunis, project, site
plan.

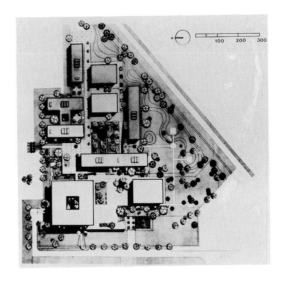

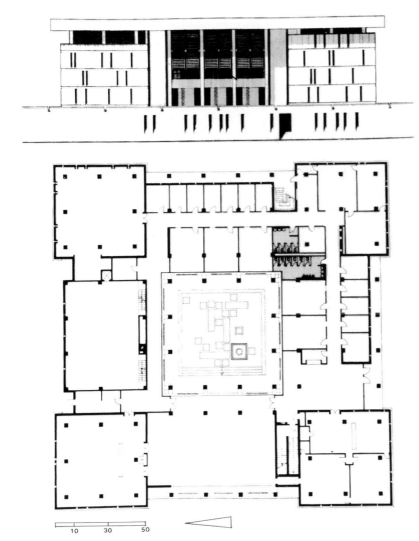

matic requirements for the spaces and the circulation system connecting them do not suggest four-sided symmetry around a central court, then why use such a form? Could it be because symmetrical, four-square massing of the exterior evokes the desired monumental effect for a government-sponsored structure? If that is the case then the decision is entirely unrelated to the way the interior of the building has been interpreted, as can be seen in its plan. Once the initial formal statement was made—four solid square corner pavilions with voids between them, the whole covered by a single independent roof plane in the shape of a square doughnut—every subsequent decision seems to have subverted the original concept.

The main entry, instead of being placed in the middle of the void facing the entry plaza and on axis with the center court, which would appear to be the logical consequence of the initial form decision, is located casually, asymmetrically, as though the classical, tripartite facade produced by the initial decision were a liability that had to be guarded against. The expression of governmental and institutional authority is clearly at odds with the manifest desire of the architect to express the ideal of a liberal education. The central court is the building's dominant space and as such demands a corresponding functional meaning. An obvious one would be the role of a circulation organizer. But the circulation system—itself a square doughnut—is shifted out of phase, and the court is left as a decorative adjunct space devoid of its expected meaning as collector of all other spaces. To further the misguidance of visual cues, there are two separate structural systems, which one might expect to articulate the pavilions and the voids between them but which instead suggest a kind of cloister walk, two of whose sides are buried among cellular classroom spaces. The ultimate symptom of structural confusion occurs at the outer four corners of the implied cloister, where one would

expect to find a structural column but instead encounters the inside corner of a pavilion envelope wall which reads as nonstructural.[17]

Perhaps the most graphic example of this kind of nonspatiality is Paul Rudolph's Natural Science Building, at the State University of New York (SUNY) College at Purchase, opened in 1976 (figs. 65, 66). The interior circulation areas imply a continuous flow of space diverted by rounded masses, very much like the flow of water between rocks, an architectural metaphor that is almost worked to death by the contoured seating in front of the building and throughout the public areas of the first floor. Yet instead of being developed into a carrier and sponsor of a host of subsequent design decisions—giving formal significance to such considerations as social and functional use, structure, lighting, and materials—the idea is allowed to degenerate into mere visual and tactile stimulation, on a par in design value with surface textures.

An example is the incongruity, in the auditorium, between the internal symmetry of access to the seating and the external asymmetry of access to the doors. The location of the building entry, with its tortured "nozzle"—a contradiction, perhaps counterpoint, to the flow idea promoted by the contour seating running up against the slatlike piers—favors one of the two identical rear entries to the auditorium, while the other point of access to the auditorium shares a comparatively cramped and obscure piece of corridor space with the elevators.[18] The result is confusion in orientation within the building, hazardous bottlenecks, and vacuous no-man's-lands—all of serious consequence in a building meant to accommodate large numbers of students hurrying to classes or lingering afterward and a rather odd failure for a circulation system full of visual cues to rush one along.

An even more significant failure lies in the social sphere. Since this is a university instruction building with considerable public traffic, one might expect the building to encourage, rather than to discourage, spontaneous encounters among students and faculty. But the design of the waiting area in front of elevators discourages chance meetings by denying that space and the areas adjacent to it any sense of spatial identity or physical amenity. Probably as a result of a purely diagrammatic treatment of the program requirements, a student lounge is provided but in considerable isolation from the most heavily used areas. It is located in a pocket carved out of a strip of laboratories and faculty offices immediately to the left of the building entry, far from the elevator waiting area and only vaguely related to the lobby and forecourt, two other potential gathering places that are further emaciated by this decision. The lobby has very little functional and formal justification beyond its pseudosymbolic role as the honorific arrival and distribution space. But even this role remains largely unfulfilled, since the building entry, auditorium access, elevators, stairs, and student lounge do not respond to it spatially. Thus the lobby and its forecourt are reduced to nearly purposeless vestiges of a classical entry sequence much as the central court in TAC's Tunis School of Law has been voided of its meaning as collector and organizer of all the spaces around it.

While in Johnson's Sheldon Memorial Art Gallery the classical entry sequence is played up to such a pitch as to make an appropriate spatial and symbolic resolution within the program limitations nearly impossible, in Rudolph's Natural Science Building the organizing powers of such a sequence are entirely unrecognized (or deliberately suppressed). In that building, if we think of the short-cycle turnover of users with their various destinations, orientation might well have benefited from the clarity of a classical sequence of spatial events. As it turns out, then, the Natural Science Building is a decorated diagram, as are, with different consequences, the Sheldon Memorial Art Gallery and the Tunis School of Law.

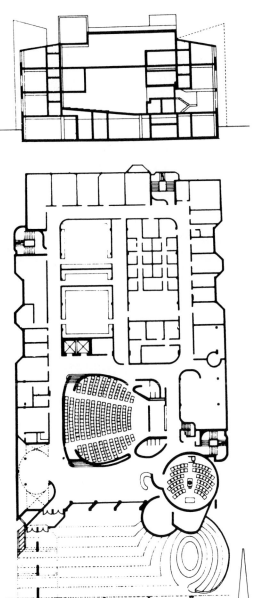

65
Paul Rudolph. Natural Science Building, State University of New York, Purchase, 1976, view of entry from mall. From *Architecture for the Arts*, The Museum of Modern Art, New York, 1971.

66
Natural Science Building, SUNY, Purchase, section and plan. From *Architecture for the Arts*, The Museum of Modern Art, New York, 1971.

20   40   60   80

67
The Architects Collaborative. John F. Kennedy Federal Building, Boston, 1961, perspective. From *Casabella*, 1965.

68
John F. Kennedy Federal Building, Boston, plan. From *Casabella*, 1965.

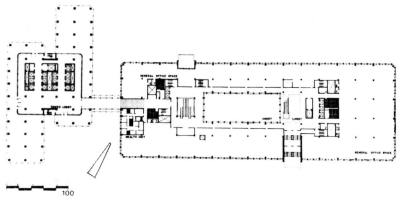

In other words, functional and visual issues are treated as if they referred to two unrelated realms of human concern instead of to one phenomenon, the experience of a building.

Among a number of other buildings by Bauhaus-legacy architects that also may be classified as decorated diagrams, though in each case for different reasons and with different consequences, are the State Services Building in Government Center, Boston, of 1961 (figs. 67, 68), and the Visual Arts Instructional Facility on the SUNY Purchase campus (figs. 69, 70), both by TAC. In the first example, the similar facades, generated by two formally contrasting plans (one a tower, the other a large horizontal building) and a connecting bridge, have been dressed up with identical patterns of deep, plastically articulated, precast mullion-and-window elements. Not only are differences in sun orientation ignored, but so are differences in perceiving from the ground the pattern elements on the vertically accentuated twenty-six-story tower, the horizontally accentuated four-story "pancake," and the one-story connecting bridge. Also ignored are the vastly different ways in which the two buildings meet the ground.

In the second example, the decoration is less literal, though equally destructive of a dialogue between plan and appearance. The disposition and size of the shed skylights, as seen in section, seem to be totally unrelated to the spaces they are to illuminate. Low, high, small, and large spaces, no matter how they are to be used, receive the same skylights, possibly for reasons of superficial unity. A more fundamental unity might have been achieved by developing a comprehensive idea of spatial organization involving all categories of spaces, rather than simply lining up all the required spaces on either side of a banal corridor. The spaces are ordered functionally, to be sure, but without regard for their implied formal structure.

A completely different version of diagram and decoration is represented by two award-winning theaters, Ulrich Franzen's Alley Theater in Houston, of 1968 (figs. 71, 72), and John Johansen's Mummers Theater in Oklahoma City, of 1972 (figs. 73–76). In both, the idea of a diagrammatic plan has been elevated to a self-conscious aesthetic. It does not remain, as in the three previous examples, on the level of neutral organizer of program functions, freeing the designer for the creation of visual interest. In fact, the diagram aesthetic of these two theaters has been tuned to the point where the diagram becomes its own decoration, so to speak, by being literally transposed into concrete, especially in the case of the Mummers Theater.

Here, to a greater extent than with the other buildings discussed so far, the issue of response to an urban context becomes important, as both theaters occupy urban grid sites (the Alley Theater's is a somewhat more distinguished one, across the street from a park). The literal articulation of all programmatic elements tends to reinforce the object quality of the buildings, thus making a spatial response to the context almost impossible. This phenomenon is particularly pronounced in the Mummers Theater, because of its Tinker Toy geometry and additive composition. In the case of the Alley Theater, on the other hand, the symmetrical disposition of the tower elements (fig. 72), especially those on the periphery, stakes out a regularized field which tends to restrain the irregularly shaped and positioned objects within it.

Still, to a greater or lesser degree, both buildings are essentially nonspatial in character. Space is either all-pervasive and passive, or a calculated, encapsulated volume. Consequently, space is not used as the mediator or articulated link between the building and its context. It might be argued, in the case of the Mummers Theater, that it has no urban context worthy of recognition. But the

69
The Architects Collaborative. Visual Arts Instructional Facility, State University of New York, Purchase, 1977, perspective. From *Architecture for the Arts*, The Museum of Modern Art, New York, 1971.

70
Visual Arts Instructional Facility, SUNY, Purchase, and section plan. From *Architecture for the Arts*, The Museum of Modern Art, New York, 1971.

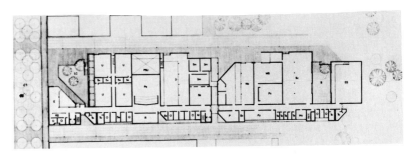

71
Ulrich Franzen. Alley
Theater, Houston, 1965–
1968. From *Process
Architecture*, 1979.

72
Alley Theater, plans. From
Process Architecture,
1979.

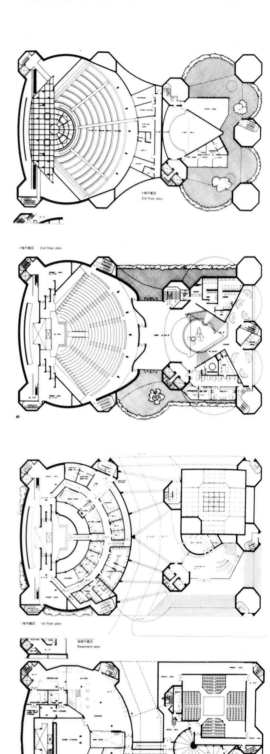

73
John Johansen. Mummers
Theater, Oklahoma City,
1967–1972 (AIA Award,
1972), exterior view.
From *Architectural
Forum*, 1968.

74
Mummers Theater, plans.
From *Architectural
Forum*, 1968.

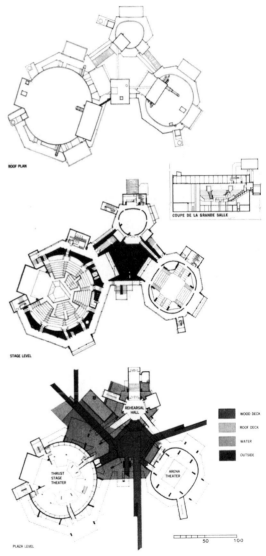

75
Mummers Theater,
exterior and interior
views. From *Architectural
Forum*, 1968.

76
Mummers Theater,
conceptual sketches.
From *Architectural
Forum*, 1968.

fault of this argument is that it either sounds too much like a license for object fixation or, taken at its most extreme, implies a rejection of the city as a coherent fabric which constitutes a physical environment conducive to a comprehensible and community-conscious urban life. Viewed thus, no urban context is unworthy of spatial recognition, for any new building, by giving off appropriate spatial cues, can help shape a context for buildings and open spaces yet to come. The history of urban architecture is in large measure the record of morphological changes based on the interaction of such spatial cues with their responses, which, in turn, become cues for future responses. Contextual insensitivity, as demonstrated by these two buildings, appears to be a particularly objectionable flaw in view of the fact that the buildings are public theaters and as such an integral part of urban life, or so one would hope.

A similar instance of contextual insensitivity is Victor Lundy's widely acclaimed Intermediate School 53 in Far Rockaway, Queens, New York, of 1968–1973 (figs. 77–81, 84, 86). Even more than Franzen's Alley Theater, though with perhaps even less justification, Lundy's school presents the physiognomy of a fortress, if not a prison. The functional rationale is probably borrowed from the popular, if murky, concept of "defensible space." It is hard to believe, however, that the proper architectural response to school vandalism is to build a fortress or, more accurately, the diagram of a fortress. The social costs alone ought to be assessed as too high for accepting such a literal response. Yet, in the context of modern architecture's fixation on the building as object, and the Bauhaus-instituted dichotomy between scientifically objective plan and artistically subjective appearance, the siting, plan, and appearance of this school become understandable if not acceptable. Rather than castigate a palpably questionable solution to the problem of

designing this New York school, it seems more illuminating to compare Lundy's I.S. 53 with what might be considered a more thoughtful and experientially richer solution built in the London area by Alan Colquhoun and John Miller about ten years earlier, in 1964 (figs. 82, 83, 85, 87–93). The school is called Secondary School, London E 15, Borough of Newham. It is meant for children of the same age group as those of the New York school.

The two schools differ vastly from one another in cultural milieu (the first, racially and linguistically mixed and with a transient and economically unstable student body, the second in all respects more homogeneous, stable, and traditional) and in size, with 1,800 pupils in the New York school as opposed to about 800 in the London school. Thus a detailed comparison makes little sense. But a comparison at the level of design principles applicable to both examples might yield some useful insights into the function of forms. As a common reference, let us recapitulate some characteristics common to any sizeable secondary school on the functional, formal, and symbolic levels.

The most important *functional* givens in any school are probably related to the movement of pupils and staff. At typical entry and exit rush time, a one-point entry (used in the New York school) may require less supervision but creates a bottleneck, while multiple entries and exists, (used in the London school) eliminate congestion but at the cost of diffusing control. Random noise outside classrooms or any other "programmed" spaces is another classic problem. Corridors, low ceilings, and hard materials increase the likelihood of a high noise level. Furthermore, besides the assigned communal spaces—gymnasium, cafeteria, or even the library—one may assume the requirement of "fieldlike" communal indoor space suitable for spontaneous play and lounging, between classes.

77
Victor Lundy.
Intermediate School 53,
Far Rockaway, New York,
1969–1973, perspective.
From *Architectural
Forum*, 1969.

78
Intermediate School 53,
exterior view. From
Architecture Plus, 1973.

79
Intermediate School 53,
interior view. From
Architecture Plus, 1973.

As to the *formal* givens, the foremost would surely revolve around a readily perceivable spatial ordering system, one that, in functional forms, will facilitate orientation and destination-finding. An equally important requirement would be a disposition of repetitive elements, such as classrooms, columns, and light sources, and their counterparts, unique elements, such as entry and singular spaces, that would aid memorization. It follows that the formal means among those at the architect's disposal, for instance, the deployment of symmetry, local and overall, would play a fundamental role.

On a third, *symbolic* level of attributes to be expected of almost any school, the one encompassing the symbolic or metaphorical appearance and the pupil's experience of the school as being at once a big house and a small city is probably the most important. Without this perception on the part of the child the indispensable sense of belonging and of active participation is difficult to foster. Measured articulation of the school's parts and subparts are its formal corollaries.

In the larger context of the neighborhood, every school naturally becomes a focus for the community—at least insofar as it consists of pupils and their parents—serving as host to parent-teacher meetings and cultural or sports events. Formally, that communal aspect would most likely affect the exterior appearance of the building and the spatial relationship to its context. The aim would naturally be to invite community participation, spontaneous or organized, thus also easing the transition from home to school and home again for the pupils. It need hardly be emphasized that this kind of symbolic formal transition is also part of the house/city perception.

Although Lundy seems concerned with this issue, as evidenced by the stepbacks between classrooms (fig. 80), other, far more powerful design decisions—from overbearing entry roof (fig. 81) to inaccessible courtyard (figs. 77, 79,

84, 86)—negate these positive intentions. Colquhoun and Miller, in contrast, by carefully calibrating access to and overlook of the assembly hall, extend the effects of the hall's reassuring singularity to every part of the school, thus allowing the house analogy of "living room" or the city analogy of "square" in a child's mind (figs. 85, 87, 92, 93).

By assigning the court space, in function and in form, to spontaneous community use and honorific school events, the New York school tries literally to interlock the school with the surrounding community. The architect's intentions fail not so much because the hydraulic steel grate across the court entrance happens to be permanently shut for pragmatic reasons, but because the fortresslike character of the building (figs. 80, 81) denotes exaggerated exclusivity of its court—as the arrival court of a medieval keep would—and casts an uneasy mystery over the other communal spaces locked within the overall volume, about 320 by 380 feet, surrounded by overpowering brick walls with hardly a window in them, four stories in height. In contrast, the London school not only gives cues from the outside as to where collective spaces might be, but offers a series of open-air transition spaces from the neighborhood to the various entrances of the school (figs. 82, 89). The fact that these controlled transition spaces occur within the sharply defined square-shaped territory of the school proper (200 by 200 feet, three to four stories in height) are largely responsible for maintaining the necessary duality of the school's identity and its outreach.

As is well known from general psychology, children, because they are more willing than adults to let their imaginations become an active part of daily life, tend to have a greater capacity to interpret spatial configurations to suit their fantasies on the one hand and their physical needs on the other (fig. 50). Given a space, or series of spaces, as intimated in the section and

80
Intermediate School 53.
From *Architecture Plus*,
1973.

81
Intermediate School 53,
entry.

other illustrations of the central hall of the London school, one can easily imagine, even as an adult, the organized morning assembly later becoming a kind of forum, implying a large scale, or alternatively, a pavilion, implying a smaller scale, each with its respective functional and symbolic connotations (figs. 88, 92, 93). Add to this the suggestion of the receding galleries as "overlooks," "cascades," and so on, and the changing natural light through the coffered roof and the number of permutations of likely associations—thought about or actually experienced—become extraordinary; there you have the stuff of rich and enriching architecture.

Yet, looking at the two schools—at least as published for the architects' peers and the public to see—one senses that the London school, although probably gelled in its design infancy into a diagrammatic formal organization, was subsequently developed into a highly resilient piece of architecture; whereas in the New York school an evidently cruder formal diagram remained essentially undeveloped, and was therefore ill-suited to take advantage of programmatic idiosyncrasies, let alone nonprogrammed spaces. Thus the "buried" cafeteria, the "detached" entrance block, and the endless corridors around the courtyard, which do not complete the expected loop and, although they tantalizingly skirt that central space, are in fact separated by glass and deep mullions from it (fig. 79): as if the child were a corporate executive resting his eyes on the court's pretty landscaping on his way to another office (fig. 78). The courtyard, rather than having been conceived as the generating space of the building, is the residue of decisions having to do much more with programmatic dispositions—three schools of 600 pupils, one to a floor, each with common facilities beneath or to the side (fig. 84).

Lundy's I.S. 53 grinds form, function, and appearance against each other, instead of unifying them by a systematic and passionate, yet lucid, examination of each decision's consequences. It is as though the various parts of the building were out of register, expressed literally in the section (fig. 84). Given the utterly asymmetrical program, a symmetrical form seems rather like a forced solution without, in its early design phase, a transformation appropriate to site and program. Symmetry is a powerful formal medium, but when used as incongruously as it is here it is reduced to a banality incapable of being the carrier, modifier, or sponsor of social, perceptual, or technological ideas. In any case, only the configuration of the envelope is given a kind of symmetry and not the spaces it hides: the lack of correspondence between envelope and content that we have seen in other Bauhaus-legacy architecture.

The architects of the London school, however, faced with the symmetrical program requirements of equal access and the same number of classrooms for boys and girls, evidently decided on a diagonally symmetrical "main component" of the whole school, incorporating all the repetitive elements, such as classrooms, in "hard walls" forming an *L* on two sides of the basic square territory, thus defining three of its four corners (fig. 85). The two extreme corners, having acquired a special quality merely on account of their formal position, are given a correspondingly special functional/symbolic meaning by the stacking of all the extra-large classrooms on top of covered, outdoor, play areas (figs. 89, 90), all directed away from the apex of the *L,* as if to project at least the ground floor spaces and their activities beyond the immediate domain of the school back toward the children's own neighborhood. (As an illustration of the apparent ease with which interdependence of function, form, and meaning are maintained in this building, the cluster of bathrooms just inside the covered play halls might be mentioned (fig. 85). Not only are bathrooms most likely to be used before and after intermission play; here they serve as spatial

82
Alan Colquhoun and John Miller. Secondary school, London, 1962–1964. From *Architectural Design*, 1965.

83
Secondary school, London. Main entry. From *Architectural Design*, 1965.

84
Victor Lundy.
Intermediate School 53,
Far Rockaway, New York,
1969–73. Section and
plans. From *Architecture
Plus*, 1973.

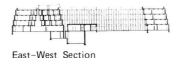

East–West Section

4

3

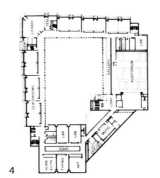

2

1

50   100

buffers between the definitiveness of the class-rooms inside and the "found space" quality of the play area outside.) Besides the two symmetrically disposed entries and locker rooms for boys and girls on the ground floor, the main public spaces (assembly, stage, and small hall), one shallow floor above, and a pair of staircases are also incorporated into the diagonally symmetrical main component.

The east and south frontiers as well as the heart of the school thus having been established, the rest of the required functions, most of them unique, can now be positioned more freely in the "hinterland," provided the square-shaped confines of the staked-out territory are observed. Thus we see the stacking of the boys' and girls' gyms in a block whose principal direction is north-south and contrary to that of the "main component," but which is tethered to the latter by a bridge, as if to signify its special place in the curriculum. In the New York school the gym block is melded into the overall mass of the building, which by the same reasoning would imply that its function and meaning are integral rather than special (fig. 84). That may be the intention, but, because the gyms are shared by all three horizontally layered schools and are accessible only from the common ground level, the pupils have, in fact, to leave their respective school levels to reach the gyms, making these spaces distinct in use as in the London school while integral in appearance. The degree of integration is further confused by the difference in layout in the corresponding area in the block containing main entry lobby, administration, and special classrooms.

A few other features of these buildings merit comparison. Where Lundy's school literally expresses diagonal quasi-symmetry by a flight of steps into the "public" court augmented by a skewed entry to the building, the diagonal organization that is apparent in the building by Colquhoun and Miller is carefully counteracted by dissolving all movement into the two perpendicular directions of the generic *L* form. The advantage of such a strategy is fairly obvious: unique and secondary spaces and volumes—gym, teachers' quarters, cafeteria, library, and so on—can be articulated with some freedom of choice and subtlety in respect to their programmatic and symbolic location within the building as a whole, as is the case with the school's gym block. Here again, subtlety means fine tuning among use, form, and meaning as understood in the context of the entire building.

The form and position of the library in the New York school (fig. 84) make it a spearhead with the classrooms trailing behind, or, perhaps, the hinge of a compass; in any case something implying great pressure, the opposite of choice and chance, commonly thought to be valuable incentives for the appreciation and private enjoyment of books. The latter seem more possible in the library of the London school (fig. 85), merely on account of its position. While it is relegated to the "hinterland," internally providing somewhat of a refuge, externally it is a proper symbolic participant in the massing of the school's north facade, which, facing the street, is the most public one. The public or honorific quality is further emphasized by its being the only space covered with a slanted roof and by an adjacent open flight of stairs leading from the street entry directly to the main level (figs. 89, 91, 92).

Upon closer inspection it can be seen that these stairs (probably not required by the program) are employed in an ingenious manner as the principal means of transition from outside to inside in both scale and meaning (figs. 92, 93). On the outside they occupy the near-center of the street facade, their position and meaning originally to have been reinforced by an unbuilt ceremonial gateway. Thus the stairs and would-be gateway serve as the focal point of an otherwise rather fractured facade. The compositional and experiential problem is that the center

North–South Section

85
Secondary school, London, section and plans. From *Architectural Design*, 1965.

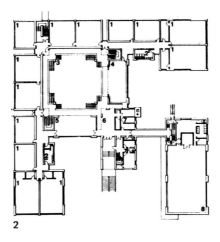

2

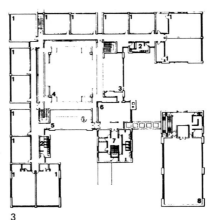

3

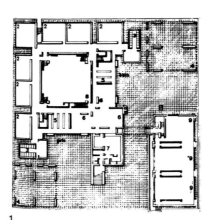

1

20 40 60

86
Intermediate School 53,
site plan. From
Architecture Plus, 1973.

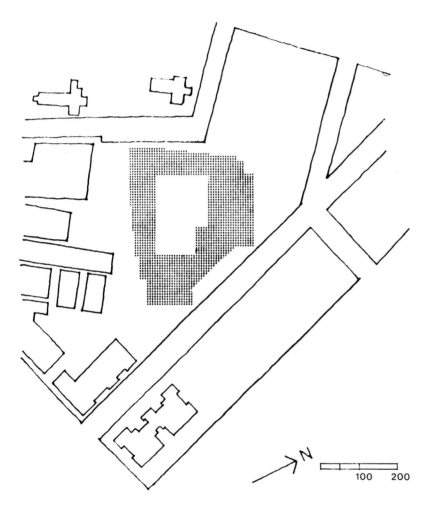

N

100   200

of the 200-foot-long facade does not coincide with the center of the major interior space, the assembly hall. Yet by a calculated series of maneuvers that seeming paradox is resolved. First, the stair is moved off the facade center, away from the gym block, so as to both reduce its classical monumentality and align it more directly with the periphery of the assembly hall (fig. 89). A grand center coalition has been translated into a more intimate edge condition. Second, providing some intimation of the drastic spatial shift to come, the adjoining wall in the direction of the assembly hall has been given a large opening, it is protected from the elements until the vestibule doors have been reached. Both of these adjustment and preparatory decisions—eastward shift of stair and eastward opening of confining wall—do more than ease the transition from a public-central to a private-peripheral setting; the entry vestibule, at the end of the stair sequence, is the first and only space one encounters which obeys and at the same time reveals the inner, diagonally symmetrical layout (fig. 93). The significance of this double interpretation is not only that a general spatial and scale transition has been achieved, but that the external orthogonal and processional axis has been translated into a diagonal axis; a literal forward thrust has been deflected to become conceptually diagonal, the imaginary sum of all internal orthogonal movement. The vestibule has thus formally become the element which, manifesting equally the attributes of use and symbol, marks the crossing of the two principal axes.

Comparing this entry sequence with the one in New York perhaps illuminates the starkest contrast between the two sensibilities at work and the sheer skill involved in bringing all levels of architectural consideration together. For an unsettling experience of contrast one need only follow the path of a pupil, teacher, or visitor from the curbside into the interior of the New York school (fig. 81). As one faces the vast garagelike portico, whose funnel shape presses one into the courtyard meant for the neighborhood public—in itself baffling—the funnel wall to the left, almost incidentally, is punctured by the main entry into lobby and school complex. Either out of wanton formalism or some perverse humor, Lundy contrived to open up a three-story slot to the sky exactly in front of the entrance doors. One is rained upon without warning, precisely at the point where most other buildings would provide shelter. Even the most elementary function of protection from the weather was sacrificed to some "greater ideal," seemingly completely at odds with the Bauhaus and Harvard/Gropius preaching.

Returning to the London school, we can see a subtlety and elegance of development similar to that shown in the 45-degree change in direction of the two major axes, though in an entirely internal example: the disposition of the direct-access stairs to the assembly hall from both the upper (honorific/visitors') and lower (utilitarian/pupils') entry levels. As can be seen in figures 85, 92, and 93, all of the eight short stairs begin in line with the inside surface of the four square "pavilion" columns, whether they lead up or down to the assembly floor. Four stairs lead up, four down. Although in plan the positions of all eight stairs appear symmetrical with respect to all diagonal and orthogonal axes, the two sets of four stairs each are, when considered spatially, symmetrical only in respect to the east–west axis of the central space. In this pattern they accept the stage space as an elaboration of the "figure" they imply by themselves, thus relegating a space very similar to the stage in size and position on the undeveloped diagram to secondary status; indeed, it is directly below the library and called the "small hall."

It hardly needs pointing out that without a split-level assembly floor—in itself likely to

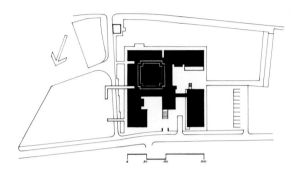

87
Secondary school, London, site plan. After architects' drawing published in *Architectural Review*, 1963.

88
Secondary school,
London, assembly hall.
From *Architectural
Review*, 1963.

89
Secondary School,
London, axonometric
views. From *Architectural
Review*, 1963.

90
Secondary school,
London, covered play
space. From *Architectural
Design*, 1965.

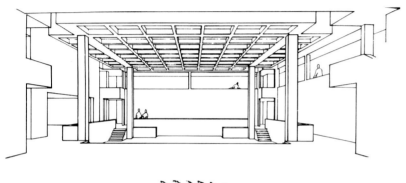

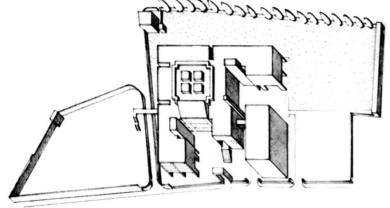

91
Secondary school,
London, model. From
Architectural Review,
1963.

92
Secondary school,
London, north-south
section. From
Architectural Design,
1965.

93
Secondary school,
London, plan perspective.
After architects' drawing
published in *Domus*,
1963.

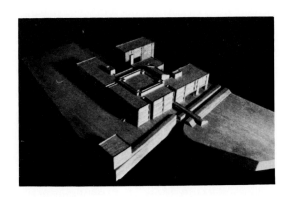

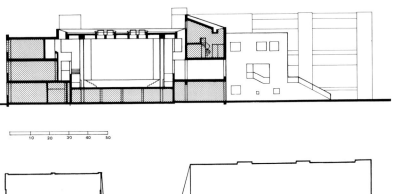

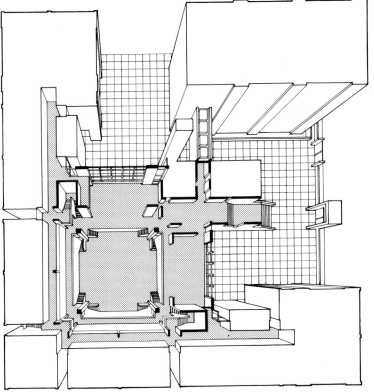

heighten the sense of pavilion and upward-receding galleries—the little charade of complementary sets of four stairs could not have taken place. Furthermore, they play a vital role in counteracting the exterior north–south axis by giving substance to an east–west axis, which emanates from the interior. Their interplay, simultaneously calibrated on symbolic, functional, and formal levels, renders the potentially tyrannical, diagonally symmetrical disposition of the "main components" not only bearable but essential to the understanding and enjoyment of this school. The diagonal organization, unlike that of the New York school, is dissolved into major and minor orthogonal orchestrated movements.

The point of this excursion has been not so much to demonstrate the obvious disparity of architectural quality between the two schools, as to show that in one case utility and the governing idea are not by principle at odds, and that in the other case the result is the very opposite of what was intended. How the second may result from a particular teaching method will be the subject of much of chapter 3.

We observed earlier in discussing Johnson's Sheldon Memorial Art Gallery how, perhaps in an overzealous attempt to break with Bauhaus antiformalism, some blatantly formal devices were employed. Symmetry and building events along a dominant axis were the two chief means identified, both denoting institutional authority. We have also noted that unqualified application of such powerful formal devices tends to inhibit spontaneous interpretation of spatial configurations for social and other purposes. This point lies at the core of much contemporary concern with the possibilities and limitations of architecture, and I will return to it in discussing the second of the next two examples: the recently completed Herbert F. Johnson Museum of Art on the campus of Cornell University by I. M. Pei, opened in 1973 (figs. 94–96), and the 1968 mas-

ter plan for the Purchase campus, SUNY, by Edward Larrabee Barnes, the bulk of it recently completed (figs. 98, 102, 104).

The most significant characteristics of Pei's museum are the symmetry and profile of its configuration, which suggest totemlike qualities and enable one to envision the building at scales ranging from an amulet on a necklace to a monument to the gods.[19] The vast, unarticulated concrete surfaces, with a smoothness achieved at great expense, materially reinforce this scalelessness. If scale is an architectural quality which permits a person to measure himself against the work and thereby grasp its relative and absolute size, and if scale depends on the calculated articulation of building parts—perhaps even on iconographically suitable but functionally extraneous elements—then Pei's museum lacks scale in almost every respect. And it is the building's totemlike ambivalence of scale which has encouraged popular interpretations of it as a "gigantic throne," a "monumental altar," of "colossal Chinese character," or, alternately, a "giant's toy" about to tumble down the hill. The randomness of popular epithets raises the suspicion that perhaps the building has no deeper meaning.

Hypothetically, meaning could exist in at least two spheres: in the physical expression of functional organization (the kind of criterion Walter Gropius would have approved of) and in the manifestation of a visual and intellectual argument addressing itself to a range of historical and cultural issues which would naturally be attached to this building on this site. The Herbert F. Johnson Museum has meaning in neither sense. With respect to the first, it presents schizoid inconsistencies, the most blatant of which is the disposition of the gallery spaces themselves. The form of the building would suggest that the north slab contains spaces of similar and perhaps repetitive use stacked on top of each other, while the spaces assembled to the south of that wall con-

94
Cornell University, Ithaca,
New York, view of
campus.

95
I. M. Pei. Herbert F.
Johnson Museum of Art,
Cornell University, Ithaca,
New York, 1969–1973.

96
Herbert F. Johnson
Museum of Art, section
and plans.

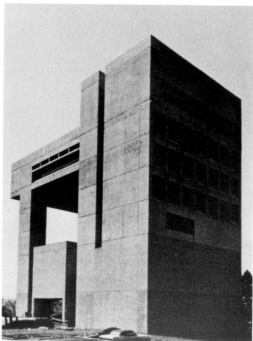

note a contrasting, perhaps unique, set of uses. It appears pointlessly contradictory that some of the gallery boxes are buried in the north slab while others are sculpturally expressed within the adjacent void. The ensuing confusion of orientation and circulation path suffered by visitors indicates that functional logic could not account for the galleries' location.

With respect to the second sphere of meaning, the building offers no contribution to the ongoing polemic of modern architecture, into which context it purports to put itself by employing a contemporary high-style vocabulary, a distillation of twenties and thirties modern movement architecture with a dash of Louis Kahn archaism. The promise of a polemic is subverted by the unsystematic, elegantly decorative, and perhaps unconscious use of formal and detailing modernist clichés such as long, horizontal window strips, vast expanses of unarticulated, "invisible" glass, and deep-set windows resulting in a brise-soleil effect. As if to mock any attempt at rational interpretation, the deep-set, sun-breaking windows principally occur on the north facade.

If the essence of a totem lies in its enigmatic character and thus in its being at once inexplicable and compelling, then the Johnson Museum, being only too explicable, not to say banal, loses all mystery and thus all essence. It is a promise unfulfilled. This conclusion is the more disturbing because it applies to so much more or less anonymous architecture being produced these days. Indeed, the Johnson Museum, together with many other similar buildings that come out of Pei's office, is taken as a model, thanks to the well-orchestrated establishment approval his work has enjoyed, as evidenced by the list of clients, the exuberant *New York Times* reviews[20], the awards, and applauding coverage in professional and other journals.

A similar criticism can be applied to the Purchase campus, by Barnes (figs. 98, 102, 104).

The consequences of employing symmetry in the service of a simplistic gestalt are, of course, far greater for a project of the size and comprehensiveness of the Purchase campus than for the relatively small and self-contained Johnson Museum, particularly since, in the case of the campus, the totem figure primarily governs plan rather than appearance. The character of an entire university has been determined by this basic design decision. Perhaps the full measure of needless damage which can be done by ignorant form making can best be seen by comparing the Purchase scheme with its prototype, Thomas Jefferson's University of Virginia, Charlottesville, of 1817–1826 (figs. 99–101, 103). In a more comprehensive comparison than this essay allows, one would, of course, have to include the archetypes of both projects, the Greek agora and the Roman forum, particularly the forum at Pompeii (fig. 97).

Although much smaller than the two modern examples (112 by 350 feet compared to about 300 by 900 feet for the Purchase platform and the University of Virginia mall[21]), Pompeii's forum is of similar proportions. Each of these spaces is meant to serve as the meeting ground for its community and each forms a diagram of buildings abutting, necklacelike, an arcade and open space. The resolution of the diagram, however, is vastly different in each case. Whereas in the forum individual buildings may be either orthogonal or tilted with respect to the arcade, thus allowing for small, irregular transition spaces (in turn allowing for unintended, informal uses) Jefferson's university is entirely orthogonal, and, although equipped with some inventive transition spaces, places them at regular intervals. Furthermore, the arcade space in the former is of different widths and physical definitions, denoting distinctions among the abutting buildings, while in the latter its very constancy (despite passage through the ten pavilions) helps make the much

97
Forum, Pompeii, about
second century B.C., plan.

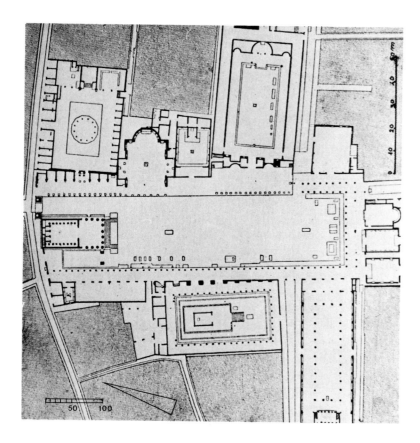

larger central space sensible as one mall. Hardly any of these characteristics and consequent attributes exist at Purchase, as we shall see in a detailed comparison to its ostensible model.

Jefferson's masterwork has for the last 150 years served as the model for innumerable campus plans across the country, so one is not surprised to recognize its shadow in this most recent attempt to gather a greater number of individually articulated, yet intricately related, university activities into a graspable whole. There are obvious organizational similarities between the two works. Each is an ensemble facing a range of lovely hills in the distance which visually close, and animate, the open end of the composition. The proportions and dimensions of the dominant quadrangle are similar, and in both cases the arcades defining the long sides are paralleled by rows of trees. By the strength of its identity, the central void in both cases is meant to allow a certain dissimilarity and freedom of local development for the perimeter buildings and their precincts without affecting the basic organization of the whole.

At the University of Virginia it is principally the gardens behind the pavilions that have benefited from this freedom, while at Purchase the fundamental idea allows the parceling out of the ten buildings attached to the arcades to different architects without risking visual chaos. It also permits each of these buildings to change and grow—within certain boundaries, of course—according to individual requirements. Apparently, to ensure the perceptual stability of the controlling figure, the four buildings at the ends of the two arcades were assigned to Barnes, the chief architect, while two other buildings flanking the major access road were awarded to the contributing architects Venturi and Rauch. Others along the platform are by Philip Johnson, The Architects Collaborative, Gunnar Birkerts, and Paul Rudolph.

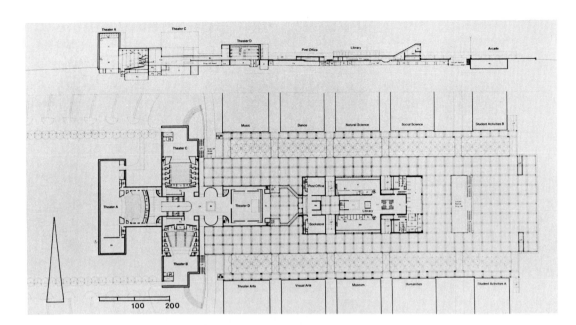

98
Edward Larrabee Barnes.
State University of New
York, Purchase, 1969–
1979, longitudinal section
and site plan. From
Architecture for the Arts,
The Museum of Modern
Art, New York, 1971.

99
Thomas Jefferson.
University of Virginia,
Charlottesville, 1817–
1826, plan.

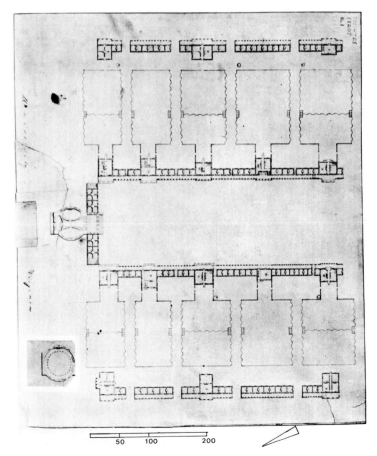

100
University of Virginia,
aerial view to south.

There is one principal programmatic difference between the conceptual model and its interpretation. While the buildings along the arcade at the University of Virginia house both teaching and living spaces (for both students and teachers), at Purchase they contain strictly departmentalized instructional facilities. Student housing is provided in two large, separate complexes immediately beyond and to either side of the open end of the quadrangle.

But the fundamental difference is spatial—a difference so great that the Purchase quadrangle can no longer be regarded as being modeled after Jefferson's "great mall" idea, but must be seen as its complete inversion, if not perversion. What at the University of Virginia is a space that gives symbolic and social meaning to the buildings surrounding it is at Purchase, a colossal totem object that leaves two relatively narrow strips of space on either side of it. Because of the peculiar quantitative relationship between totem figure and quadrangle ground, the space surrounding the central object is perceived as left over, devoid of identity (figs. 98, 102). It is this lack of spatial identity—as we have already observed in two of the perimeter buildings, notably Rudolph's Natural Science Building—that discourages a sense of place and consequently deters spontaneous encounters—as if social interaction were to be allowed only in specifically programmed spaces. There is only one of these spaces that allows any degree of spontaneity (because it is an optional outdoor space), the one defined by the east end of the theater complex and the opposing face of the post office, bookstore, and library mass (figs. 98, 102).

The lack of a twenty-four-hour cycle of activities in the quadrangle (all residences being sequestered on two separate minicampuses) demands a particularly sensitive architectural effort to render it and its periphery responsive to spontaneous use. Scale, as defined in the critique of

the Herbert F. Johnson Museum, would surely be a most important aspect of that effort. The articulation of transitions between indoor and outdoor spaces, bright and dark ones, busy and empty ones, large and small ones, upper and lower levels, hard and soft ground surfaces, and so on would further encourage total use of the building complex. By total use I mean functional, social, and intellectual use, the last category being the most challenging one and usually the one that makes a work of art memorable and emotionally moving. The University of Virginia has met that challenge well; SUNY at Purchase has not.

Instead of a sense of scale and clear transitions we have yet another Bauhaus-legacy built diagram, in all its schematic brittleness, in this case masquerading in neoclassic serenity.[22] Despite the schematic qualities of the external form, its placement, and the character and layout of its internal spaces (observe the collision of theaters at the head of the totem), the central complex of buildings is perhaps less of a failure, according to the criteria listed above, than the two arcades connecting the instructional buildings. A glance at the architect's rendering of the arcade as seen by someone walking in it (fig. 104) would probably convince anyone that the deliberate articulation of space and mass in the service of comprehensive use was not high on the list of objectives. It is doubtful whether such an essentially humanistic term as *arcade* should even be used to describe that uninviting passageway.[23] Moreover, the interface between arcade and adjacent buildings could not be more brutal. The abruptness might have been partly softened by astute responses on the part of each building, but most of them fail to meet this demand, judging from those that have gone up so far and from published drawings of those that have not yet been built. Also, the quadrangle—a monumental, flat, mostly hard-surfaced platform—ob-

103
University of Virginia,
Charlottesville, view
within arcade.

104
SUNY, Purchase,
perspective within arcade.
From *Architecture for the
Arts*, The Museum of
Modern Art, New York,
1971.

literates the site's natural gentle slope and thus needlessly aggravates the problems involving scale, transition, spontaneous use, and so forth, brought about by other design decisions. There is a good Bauhaus explanation for the platform: it permits the unimpeded and protected distribution of services among all the buildings touching it to occur below grade level. But a functional justification alone, as compelling as it might be, is insufficient reason for a decision of such importance.

At Purchase, contradictory design decisions are camouflaged by means of architectural cosmetics, giving an appearance of simplicity, indeed, almost banality. By contrast, one is immensely impressed by the real simplicity and economy of design means with which Jefferson achieved a spatially and symbolically rich campus. He employed three principal means. First, he terraced the great mall (officially called the Great Lawn), thus giving it a preferred direction and a certain amount of inherent scale by causing the arcades to follow the cascading movement of the land and breaking the originally 900-foot-long walk into rhythmic intervals (fig. 101).

Second, in Jefferson's complex the interlocking of arcade and pavilions makes the arcade itself into the interface between mall and buildings, in contrast with Purchase, where the interface is reduced to an imaginary plane at the outer edge of the arcade. At the University of Virginia, the concept of interface is given spatial expression and intellectual meaning by the creation of deliberate ambiguity within the arcade, which offers the observer multiple interpretations of his own relationship to the community. When passing under a pavilion the observer has two simultaneous spatial experiences (fig. 103). While looking straight ahead he is in the arcade tube, impelled to continue moving tangentially to the quadrangle. With his back to the pavilion entrance, looking out over the quadrangle past much larger columns placed out of line with the arcade colonnade which seem to rise as freely skyward as the nearby tree trunks, he finds himself in a porchlike space projecting perpendicularly into the quadrangle. The observer can control and choose whichever interpretation to be conscious of, or blend the two at will, because each interpretation has its clearly defined spatial identity. Put differently, the choice is between the anonymity of the arcade and the prominence of the pavilion, or anywhere along the spectrum established by these two metaphors, according to the observer's emotional and intellectual frame of mind at the moment. Thus the architecture can become one's own in an intellectual and emotional sense which transcends literal possession.

The third of Jefferson's principal means of giving spatial and symbolic expression to scale and transition are the arcade and pavilion columns themselves, more specifically their shape, size, proportion, spacing, and surface treatment. A different choice of transition element between arcade and mall—for instance, square columns or thin ones at large intervals—would have produced a dramatically different spatial effect, one which would have precluded the sense of ambiguity created by interlocking pavilions and arcade. The inadequate realization of this idea, so full of possibilities, would have limited the result to a diagram, which is precisely what happened at Purchase.

In the group of buildings discussed so far, plan and appearance can be based on a multitude of relationships, depending on whether the intention is *single* (be it holistic or ironic) and carried through, as in the works by Le Corbusier, Aalto, Schinkel, Colquhoun and Miller, or Jefferson, or *twofold,* but lacking sufficient conceptual and experiential links to hold the building together. Works in the latter category were analyzed singly, in pairs, or in comparison to works of the former category to reveal the nature of missing links, as a way of describing the process by which the plan as diagram diverged from appearance as decoration. The result was a decorated diagram in the case of Breuer's house, Johnson's and Franzen's apartment houses, Johnson's museum, Rudolph's campus building, Lundy's school and TAC's office and campus buildings; a totemized diagram in the case of Barnes's campus and Pei's museum; and a concretized diagram in the case of Franzen's and Johansen's theaters. Whether the diagram is decorated, totemized, or concretized, a fundamental split between plan and appearance, and often between interior and exterior, remains as the central fact in Bauhaus-legacy buildings. (See table on p. 97.)

My principal argument is that architectural training at Harvard under Gropius and Breuer strongly promoted—unconsciously, perhaps—the kinds of design decisions that shaped the buildings discussed. Aside from actual student work produced in Gropius's and Breuer's studios, which would require patient historical research to find and catalog (for another kind of study), the best evidence to substantiate my thesis is curriculum objectives, as conveyed explicitly and implicitly, intentionally and unintentionally, in the catalog descriptions of courses and in the formulations of studio problems.

A closer examination of one of these, a sketch problem given to the master's class in 1950 by Gropius (assisted by Benjamin Thompson) and again, in slightly altered form, in 1951 (assisted by William Lyman), reveals an underlying design attitude that informed both school problems and commissioned buildings. The 1951 version, "Site Development for Family Residences" (see appendix A.1) includes the following instructions:

The student is asked to select a 3-bedroom house of his liking, one he has designed or a plan by another, and on the site chosen explore the possibilities of achieving *visual variety* [italics mine] by such means as the following:
a. Use alternately the plan as well as its mirror.
b. Place the house at different angles to the sun.
c. Alternate the materials, their textures and colors, and alternate the bright and dark effect.
d. Confine the adjacent outdoor living space around the house by varying combinations of pergolas, trellis [sic], screens, hedges, fences, shrubs, and groups of trees.
e. Place the garage or car port at different angles to the house.
f. Add a screen porch to the house at different positions and angles.

To a large degree this means thinking creatively more about the spaces outside the house than those inside. The blunt extreme, where seemingly the former are never thought about, is the average speculative development which in growing numbers obliterates the American landscape.[24]

Presumably, the exercise is meant to stimulate the formulation of an answer to the deplored "average speculative development." It contains an invitation to think creatively about surrounding spaces, to be sure, but on what level, using what means? By considering exterior spaces as potential extensions of interior spaces? By considering the spaces defined between two or more houses? No! The clue given the student is a list of pattern and texture elements pertaining to a *single* house in which house, garage, porch, trellises, hedges, and surface materials all assume equal importance. A preoccupation with pattern and texture seems to govern all scales from the site plan to the wood grain of a trellis. The very lack of hierarchy among the items on the list confirms that preoccupation.

In point *d* the student is asked to confine outdoor areas. But instead of directing him to principles by which this might be done, such as degrees and methods of spatial enclosure, the exercise gives him a shopping list of predetermined objects and surface treatments. There is no reason for the student, following these instructions, to go beyond achieving a nice arrangement of objects and surface elements in the service of "visual variety," for he is asked to provide optical stimulation almost as an end in itself. The presentation requirement of "perspective sketches showing the variety of appearances in spite of using the same house type"[25] reinforces that attitude. Thus, what was meant as an exercise in "reconciling the economic advantages of mass production of standardized building parts with man's desire for individuality"[26]—a rather good objective, then and now—turned out to be a prescription for almost meaningless production of visual variety. The disturbing conclusion one must draw from this example is that the student was required to do no more than a

visually appealing alternative to the speculator's development, the antithesis of the stated objective of the problem, while he was led to believe that he was bringing the world—or at least the American suburbs—one step closer to Bauhaus perfection. The reputation of his professor alone would have had him believe that.

The apparent contradiction between intentional and unintentional objectives has even larger implications. It is in a student problem like this one that we can perceive the seeds of formalism, in the pejorative sense as the term is commonly being used, that is, connoting the employment of forms for purely literal and superficial reasons such as visual variety. Formalism in this sense implies a total nonrecognition of the multiplicity of meanings a form may have: intrinsically, as part of a structure or system of forms or a fragment of imagined or real wholes; iconographically, as a cultural symbol; and empirically, as a functional clue. One could, of course, make a case *for* formalism as connoting the deliberate employment of forms in the service of a larger conception of architecture which permits forms to function as repositories and generators of all levels of meaning—as agents of formal structure. Such an inversion would imply a recognition of certain immutable formal characteristics which are inherent in any form—solid or void—and its capacity, by means of formal analogies, to sponsor human activity, physical structure, and construction techniques rather than be their by-product. As we have seen, Jefferson's University of Virginia is a vivid example of this kind of positive formalism, as are Colquhoun and Miller's school in London, Schinkel's Altes Museum in Berlin, Aalto's Villa Mairea in Finland, and Le Corbusier's Errazuris house in Chile, as well as his villa in Vaucresson. Main Street is also a good example.

Expanding our search for clues to possible curriculum intentions (both explicit and implicit) beyond the examination of one representative master's class problem, we can identify three characteristics which permeate the curriculum as it is represented in the official course descriptions (see appendix B) and in a random selection of master's class problems. The first is an explicit *commitment to architecture in the service of democratic ideals*; the second is an implicit *preference for suburbia* over the city as the proper locale for human habitation; and the third is a *bias in favor of pragmatism*. These form an underlying value structure, a philosophical and aesthetic attitude toward architectural design with a concomitant distrust of history and theory. (All three characteristics are evident, in varying degrees of intensity and mixture, in the work of the Harvard graduates discussed earlier.) Anyone familiar with Gropius's writings, as collected in *Scope of Total Architecture*, will understand these attitudes as a further expression of beliefs which he never tired of asserting all through his Bauhaus and Harvard years. There is, of course, some irony in finding such a sharply delineated attitude permeating a curriculum which was meant to foster open-mindedness among its students. As Walter Gropius said when he took over the chairmanship at Harvard: "It is not so much a ready-made dogma that I want to teach, but an attitude towards the problems of our generation which is unbiased, original and elastic."[27]

Perhaps the very loftiness of such ideals increases the distance between intention and solution by loading from the start heavy burdens of conscience and social responsibilities on every design decision. All the more so since generalized, abstract goals do not by definition lend themselves to interpretation and transformation in designing buildings. On the other hand, models, be they buildings, trees, or poems, equipped with their formal structures, permit, as we have seen, the invention of analogous formal structures suited to the task at hand. It was Gropius's wish, it seems, to eliminate the notion of the model altogether. Yet the human proclivity to

perceive and think in object (model) terms made his directives vague and the field for design action foggy. Models or model types, at least architectural ones, are unlikely to be suggested in a studio problem conceived of an antihistorical attitude, for the very concept of modeling relies on precedent, if not on history in an academic sense. Memory as much as aspiration is touched by models, making a structured yet individualized design process possible. Yet, despite the history-free appearance of the design directives given to Harvard students, which implied the possibility, if not the certainty, of entirely original solutions, two types—"good" modern movement buildings and "bad" academic buildings—could still insinuate themselves into the problem formulation, thereby undercutting the intended aim.

The *commitment to architecture in the service of democracy* comes through most explicitly in some of the preambles to studio problems concerned with public buildings. In the introduction to a library problem, for example, the student is told that "the Library is not only a place for recreation and information but potentially an instrument for the formation of 'The New Democrat.'"[28] In another problem, the stipulated art museum is to be a "vital living force in the city and the building that houses it should honestly express that quality."[29] The student is reminded that the "overall clients are men, women, and children of the city who will either reap a harvest of learning and appreciation of art from the center or will avoid it as a great dead monument erected to the ego of the designer."[30]

The social consciousness evident in most program formulations finds its expression in the curriculum leading to a bachelor of architecture degree in the form of a strong planning component in the first year. On the level of professional involvement, the democratic idea of teamwork is given a foundation through the identical course work required in the first year for architecture, landscape architecture, and city planning students and is given substance by the one-semester requirement of practical experience. As students worked on the job with a contractor or architect, the virtues of teamwork were to reveal themselves, aside from the practical benefits of taking part in the building process (fig. 105).

Perhaps the most obvious indication of a *preference for suburbia* over the city is the preponderance of suburban problems given in Gropius's master's class. Among a dozen such problems from the years 1946–1951 (among the few that survive in the GSD library) only three have urban settings (a library, a museum, and a graduate student center), while eight have suburban settings and one is rural. The suburban problems cover the range of typical suburban activities: homemaking (in detached single-family residences), education (in nursery and elementary schools), shopping (in a supermarket), and recreation (in a restaurant in the country and in an art center). Although not stated explicitly, it is strongly implied in the formulation of most of these problems that the suburban and rural life is healthier for mind and body and certainly more democratic than life in the city. With such an indifferent, if not escapist, attitude toward the city being promoted at school, one can hardly expect sympathetic, enlightened treatment of urban architectural problems by architects trained in such an anticity ethos. Yet, as it happened, many inner cities across the United States were in dire need of repair and renewal at just about the time, in the fifties and early sixties, when most of the Harvard graduates we have been discussing achieved enough prominence to be given significant urban commissions.

In light of the postwar migration to suburbia and redoubled enthusiasm for suburban life throughout America, it is easy to see how Gropius and his school could have been swept up in the current trend. But another reason why Gropius neglected the city as habitat may have been

that he held history—whose continuity is embodied in and symbolized above all by cities—in low esteem.

More specifically, it would certainly be unfair to put the entire blame for the much-lamented failures of urban renewal and other failures of inner city redevelopment, in the fifties and sixties, on Walter Gropius's pedagogy in the forties. We can be sure, however, that the value structure and the conceptual tools which were taught and otherwise promoted at Harvard under Gropius and Breuer prepared their students poorly for urban tasks. We can also be sure, as pointed out in chapter 1, that architecture schools throughout the country were likely to take their cues from Harvard after the arrival of the founder of the Bauhaus, the only established school where modern architecture had been taught. In evaluating the architectural events of the decade 1929–1939 at a Columbia University symposium in 1964, Vincent Scully observed: "Modern architecture, as it had developed and was being taught in America by the late thirties, was small in scale, antimonumental and urbanistically destructive. Despite the sociological pronouncements of its pedagogues it was, in fact, neither functional nor structural in its methods and its forms. Instead it was pictorial."[31]

But let us return to the discussion of the Gropius curriculum and some of its studio problems. In introducing an elementary school problem, Gropius calls on Ralph Waldo Emerson, his neighbor of sorts (Lincoln and Concord, their respective domiciles, are neighboring townships in Massachusetts), to bear witness to his own belief in the necessary re-creation of The Natural Man, uncorrupted by the economic, political, and aesthetic evils of the city. Emerson, quoted in Gropius's preamble to a master's class problem, put it this way: "Rather let us have men whose manhood is only the continuation of their boyhood, natural characters still; such are able and fertile for heroic action; and not that sad spectacle with

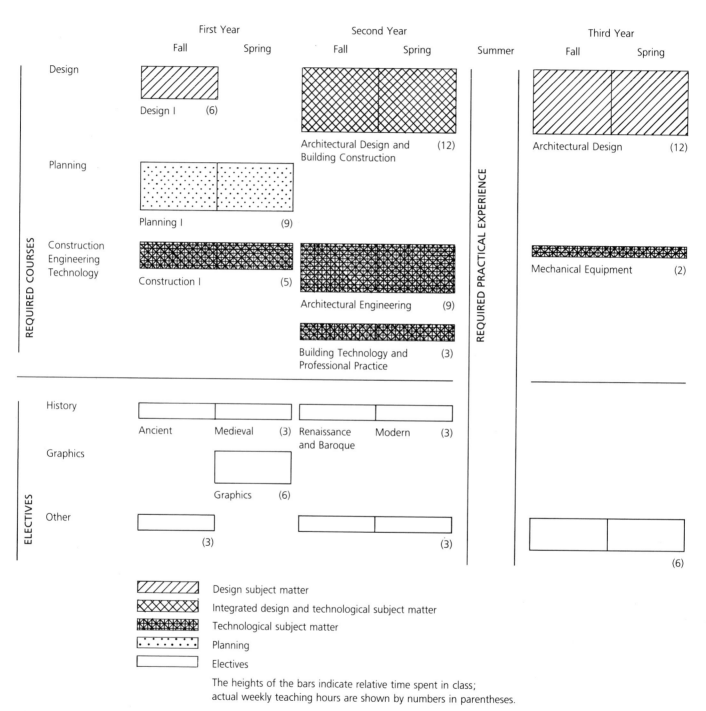

The heights of the bars indicate relative time spent in class;
actual weekly teaching hours are shown by numbers in parentheses.

105
Typical curriculum in
architecture (B. Arch),
Graduate School of
Design, Harvard
University, 1946–1947.

which we are all too familiar, educated eyes in uneducated bodies"[32] (see appendix A.2). Talking about teamwork, Gropius describes the requisite attitude as that held by "a man who has been able to empty his mind of prejudice and all non-essential considerations and has thereby arrived at a state of *new innocence* [italics mine] which allows him to penetrate to the very core of his task."[33] And, on a historical level, he says quite optimistically: "The morphology of dead styles has been destroyed and we are returning to honesty of thought and feeling."[34] In fact, viewing his career as a whole one could almost say that Gropius was obsessed with the mission of returning to mankind its paradisical innocence—a pursuit somewhat at odds, it would seem, with the encouragement of technological progress.

Here the third of the curriculum characteristics, a *bias in favor of pragmatism,* may be taken to represent the "corrupt" half of the paradox, technology in all its mutations. But this leads us far beyond the aims of this essay. It is probably the emphasis on a pragmatic approach to architectural design, so apparent in the official curriculum description and in the formulations of master's class problems (see appendixes) that accounts for the high degree of technical competence that characterizes most of the work built by Harvard graduates of the Gropius/Breuer years. As mentioned in chapter 1, their early houses, in particular, became famous for their high standard of technical quality and firmly established the reputations of their designers, especially among potential clients, as good architects. In the introduction to *Scope of Total Architecture,* Gropius explains his admiration for Yankee pragmatism as opposed to European reflectiveness in the following manner:

I have found throughout my life that words and, particularly, theories not tested by experience, can be much more harmful than deeds. When I came to the U.S.A. in 1937 I enjoyed the tendency among Americans to go straight to the practical test of every new-born idea, instead of snipping off every new shoot by excessive and premature debate over its possible value, a bad habit that frustrates so many efforts in Europe. This great quality should not get lost in favor of biased theorizing and fruitless, garrulous controversy at a moment when we need to muster all our strength and originality in trying to keep creative impulses active and effective against the deadening effect of mechanization and overorganization that is threatening our society.[35]

Small wonder, then, that Gropius's prescription for the proper academic format is analogous to that of an architectural office. In "Blueprint of an Architect's Education," he says, "The more the collaboration between teachers and students resembles office practice, the better."[36] The same idea of a practical approach also finds expression in the stated objectives of the third-year architectural design studio taught by Breuer and two associates in the bachelor of architecture sequence:

To facilitate the student's approach in design and to make it direct and creative, the physical planning of each problem is preceded by a diagrammatic study of the functions. The problems closely follow the actual practice of the architect-designer by introducing clients, contractors and authorities concerned.[37]

The work to be done in Gropius's master's class is similarly described:

This work will comprise major problems in architectural design and planning. Four such problems are offered each year. These problems will include:
a. the research necessary for the gathering of social and economic data;
b. the detailing of structural elements and of installation;
c. the computation of financing and of operational cost of buildings;
d. the study of professional practice (specifications, documents, legal problems).[38]

In looking at this simple list of objectives, it appears that the pursuit of pragmatism has become so literal, not to say ideologically obsessive, as to drive considerations of design development on the levels of idea, form, and social content out of existence. The study of precedents, on the level of models and formal structures, as possible resources for design development, is consequently also missing from the list, and there is, indeed, no mention anywhere in the catalog of history as part of an architect's education. It merely appears as a possible elective, almost as a vestige from another era, on the roster of courses (fig. 105). In the face of Gropius's legendary ideological opposition to the cultivation of a historical consciousness, this discovery comes as no surprise.

As described in the GSD catalog, the design process has become a mysterious quantum jump from research to detailing to computation, reminiscent of Hannes Meyer's famous diagram "The Plan Calculates Itself from the Following Factors" (fig. 106). The mystery is only compounded by the explicit claim in Breuer's studio description that such neutral design activities—presumably immunized against personal interpretation—are meant to make the student's approach in design "direct and creative." The implied opposition between impersonal research and implementation on the one hand and the promotion of a personal approach to design on the other may be obvious to today's reader of the 1946–1947 GSD catalog, but it almost certainly went unnoticed by students in the forties. Innocence versus progress has thus been recast as self-expression versus scientific objectivity. One is strongly tempted to find the pedagogical roots of the fatal nondiscourse between plan and appearance of so many buildings designed by prominent Harvard graduates in the attitude expressed in these two course descriptions.

That same posture of hard-nosed pragmatism at the expense of intellectually speculative and architecturally contextual investigations characterizes almost all of the available problem descriptions, among them "A Graduate Center for Harvard University" (see appendix A.3), given in 1948 as the terminal nine-week studio assignment in Gropius's master's class (figs. 107, 108). The program, site, and circumstances were evidently borrowed from TAC, where Gropius and his partners were working on what was to become the world-renowned Harvard University Graduate Center. But what is of interest here is less the built solution by TAC than the formulation of objectives for the master's students' guidance. The programmatic complexities of sponsorship and use are spelled out in great detail, as are the demands of construction and operating economy. Those demands are, in fact, elevated to the top of the list of design priorities. But even at the bottom of the list there is not a word about the physical and historical context within which this complex of buildings is to exist, even though the Harvard campus is one of urban America's historically and contextually most charged places (fig. 108). Even the sole reference to the designing of spaces for appreciative use is cloaked in the language of pseudoscientific pragmatism:

The final solution to the problem must, therefore, be based on finding a balance between the relatively rigid requirements of economy and construction, and the *less definable psychological requirements which, when met, provide a stimulating environment for education* [italics mine].[39]

The entire range of meanings—perceptual, symbolical, and historical—which spaces and objects are capable of having has been conflated into "psychological requirements," which, assumed to be measurable, are relied upon to create a stimulating environment. The philosophy of functional pragmatism has at last found its aesthetic corollary.

In a larger, historical frame of reference, the unrelenting, if ultimately naive, pursuit of literal

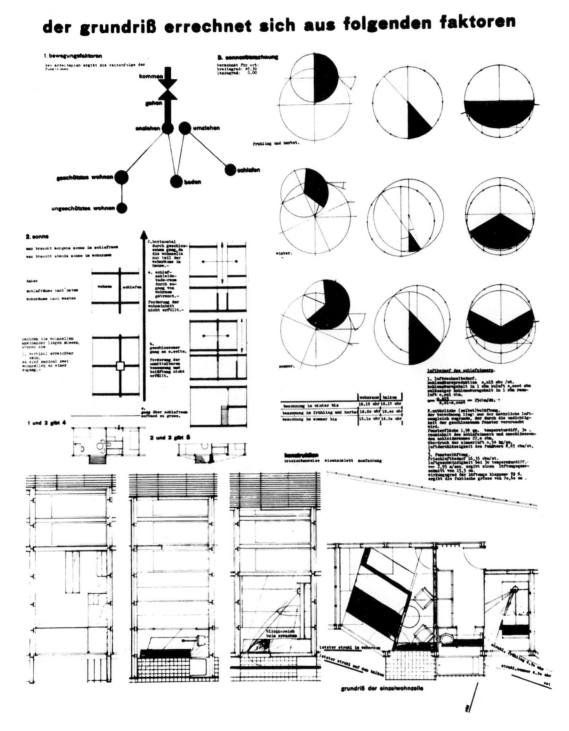

106
Hannes Meyer. "The Plan
Calculates Itself from the
Following Factors."
Bauhaus, Dessau, 1930.

107
The Architects Collaborative. Harvard University Graduate Center, Cambridge, Massachusetts, 1949–1950.

108
Harvard University Graduate Center, plan showing location on campus, 1965.

200   400   800

and presumed measurable cause-and-effect relationships within pairs of architectural entities
may very well be among the most destructive of
Bauhaus contributions to architectural design.
Gustav Hassenpflug's bridge of 1927, for exper-
iencing by touch the vibrations, pressures, and
textures of various materials (fig. 109), is only the
most vivid example of a host of attempts at mea-
suring and then graphically codifying tactile experiences which invited one to predict a desired
haptic response from the subject. It is only a small
step from the prediction of a real haptic response
caused by running one's fingers across some textures to the manipulation of pseudotactile responses caused by looking at rough and smooth,
soft and hard surfaces.

John Johansen's United States Embassy in Dublin (1957–1963) (figs 110, 111) and Paul Rudolph's much-published Graphic Arts Center
housing project for the lower West Side of Manhattan (1967; figs. 112, 113) are prominent examples of an insistence on the pseudotactile
involvement of the viewer/user or subject. Belonging generally to the category of decorated
diagram, the embassy presents an exterior which
is almost literally a transposition into precast concrete of a Celtic basket-weave pattern.[40] The
same pattern is repeated on the inside of the
ring-shaped building, facing the circular court.
While the embassy's exterior evokes the tactile
experience of the actual weave of a basket or
cloth—as incompatible as that image may be
with the load-bearing function of the enormous
precast units—the exterior of Rudolph's huge
housing structure evokes childhood's tactile joys
of piling up building blocks, where the resulting
form is more or less arbitrary.

Both projects suffer from problems of scale
because they so literally represent an additive
process borrowed from small-scale handiwork.
They seem like small, toylike things blown up to
gigantic size. There is no hierarchy of scale rela-

109
Gustav Hassenpflug.
Model illustrating tactile
experience in vibration
and pressure, and its
graphic representation.
Bauhaus, Dessau, 1927.

110
John Johansen. United
States Embassy, Dublin,
1957–1963, view. From
Architectural Forum,
1964.

111
United States Embassy,
Dublin, plan. From
Architectural Forum,
1964.

112
Paul Rudolph. Graphic
Arts Center, New York,
project, 1967,
photomontage.

113
Graphic Arts Center
project, detail of model.

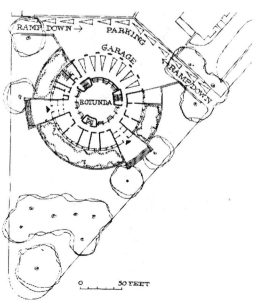

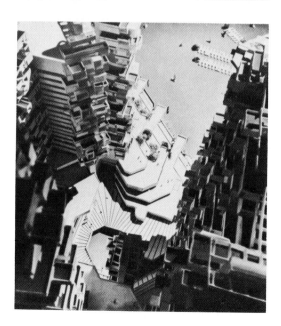

tionships between the details and the building as a whole which would enable one to relate to the building and in turn to relate the building to its context. This deficiency is particularly glaring in the Graphic Arts Center project (fig. 112), where the comprehension of the city depends on the apprehension of articulated scale shifts. Traditionally, these are represented in the city as a series of hierarchic relationships of part and whole: the front door is to the building as the building is to the block and the block is to the district. In other words, the unrestrained redundancy of surface texture—optically exciting though the play of light and shade might be—tends to make this project, like the Dublin embassy appear as the random fragment of a greater whole, though without ironic intent; the additive knitting or piling process seems simply to have stopped temporarily. A more recent example of the same concept may be seen in Philip Johnson's I.D.S. Center in Minneapolis (1972; figs. 114, 115). By jiggling the envelopes of four discrete buildings, an amorphous space is made to emerge between them. "Visual pleasure" is provided by some hanging glass modules of indeterminate scale. These are the three-dimensional equivalent of the pseudotactile plan, creating flux and irritation at the same time. Rest is not to be found. There appears to be little programmatic or contextual justification for such fragmentation. Rather, one suspects that "knitting," "piling," and pseudotactility are the unintended by-product of a design attitude that has its roots in the pedagogical concept of the pleasure principle, a time-honored inducement to experimentation and learning given exaggerated prominence in the Bauhaus ethos.[41]

László Moholy-Nagy, in his foreword to *The New Vision*, quite explicitly refers to the use of the pleasure principle in Bauhaus education: "It is the practical exercise and the pleasure in sensory experiences which lead [the student] to a security of feeling and later to the creation of

114
Philip Johnson. IDS Center, Minneapolis, Minnesota, 1972, interior view. From *Architectural Forum*, 1973.

115
IDS Center, ground level plan. From *Architectural Forum*, 1973.

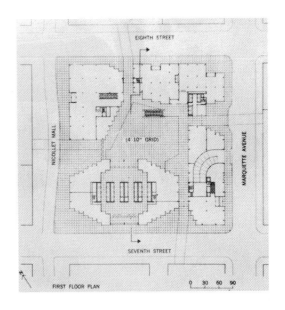

objects which will satisfy human needs which are spiritual as well as utilitarian."[42] Gropius himself advocates the following intent and format for an "Experimental Workshop and Preliminary Design Course":

This training should start with a general pre-liminary course aimed at co-ordinating the elements of handwork and design. . . . The student should be introduced, first, there-fore, to three-dimensional experiments; that is, to the elements of "building," i.e., com-position in space with all sorts of experi-ments in materials. For example, observing the contrast between rough and smooth, hard and soft, tension and repose, will help the student to discover for himself by exer-cise of his hands the peculiarities of materi-als, their structure and textures. Working with materials, the student begins simulta-neously to understand surface, volume, space and color. In addition to technical skill, he develops his own form language in order to be able to give visible expression to his ideas. After he has absorbed the elementary studies, he should then be ready to attempt compositions of his own invention.[43]

Gropius's stated aim for this first encounter with architectural elements is to give the student self-confidence—Moholy-Nagy's "security of feel-ing"—the intention being "to widen the person-ality rather than to provide professional skill."[44] The latter disclaimer seems to be in curious con-tradiction to the acquisition of technical skill. But a far more serious confusion of claims is con-tained in Gropius's ideas about generating form; evidently the student is to "develop his own *form language* [italics mine]" by manipulating materi-als and textures. That, in my view, is not form manipulation but tectonics. Aside from being a rather narrow and barren basis for a personal style with which to "attempt compositions of his own invention," this misconception about form illustrates how easily the pleasure principle can be parlayed into a method of genuine invention, in this case the invention of form. But perhaps

the greatest danger of the pleasure principle, in pedagogical terms, is that it induces a kind of narcotic fascination with mindless graphic and tectonic activity (particularly if given legitimacy by a history of pseudoscientific experiments like Hassenpflug's bridge).

Admittedly, it is often tempting for the teacher, student, or practitioner to employ the pleasure principle as a kind of overall justifier, either in the process of making a design or in speculating on its effects on a hypothetical be-holder. The glib rationale that what *feels* good *is* good is all too often used as an excuse for not thinking through the many-layered conse-quences of one's design decisions. That sort of thinking, however, presupposes the acceptance of the designer's will as a critical force in the design process. It is, moreover, precisely this kind of exercise of will, which the Gropius scheme of education tries to reject that accounts, in large part, for the exaggerated importance of the plea-sure principle in the Bauhaus ethos.

The rejection, or at least the distrust, of volition in the design process finds its reinforcing coun-terpart in the neutralization of perception of the design—as well as any other visual phenomena—in Gropius's scheme of things. Although there are recurrent, if rather vague, references to "creativity," "inspirational spark," and a "new language of vision" throughout Gropius's writ-ings, in particular, his essay "Blueprint of an Ar-chitect's Education,"[45] the act of seeing is fundamentally assumed to be (or perhaps desired to be) an objective, measureable process with codifiable causes and effects (fig. 116). We know, of course, as any up-to-date textbook on perception psychology will stress, that seeing is a highly value-laden process involving uncon-scious, as well as conscious, decision making by the viewer.

Certainly the most spectacular evidence of Gropius's belief in the objectivity of vision con-

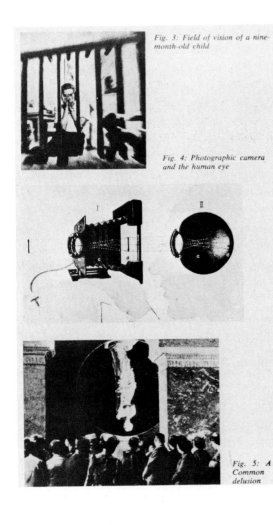

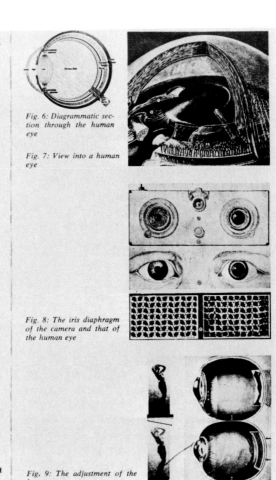

Fig. 3: Field of vision of a nine-month-old child

Fig. 4: Photographic camera and the human eye

Fig. 5: A Common delusion

Fig. 6: Diagrammatic section through the human eye

Fig. 7: View into a human eye

Fig. 8: The iris diaphragm of the camera and that of the human eye

Fig. 9: The adjustment of the human eye

116
Walter Gropius.
Illustrations comparing human sight to a stereoscopic camera.
From *Scope of Total Architecture*, Collier Books, New York, 1962.

117
Gropius, the eye
compared to a camera,
from *Scope of Total
Architecture.*

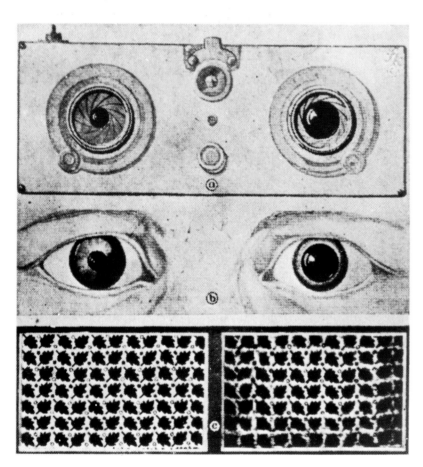

sists of the double page of images he selected to illustrate his point about the eye being like a camera in *Scope of Total Architecture* (figs. 116, 117). Inevitably, this kind of literal parallel between eye and camera stresses the mechanical aspects of perception at the expense of the intellectual and emotional aspects, such as the influence of memory, anticipation, and critical attitude on what one sees and how one sees it. In short, seeing is anything but objective; it is subjectively selective. Seeing is judging.

The Gropius/Harvard course structure, course descriptions, and studio problem formulations deliberately encourage a search for fresh solutions derived from analysis of given facts, thus discouraging, if not preventing, equally deliberate use of analogous precedents. It appears, however, that when the eye is systematically denied as the first judge in designing architecture, hosts of more or less impulsive, insufficiently examined, and nonetheless appropriate visual analogs (precedents, models, prototypes) intrude into the design anyway, because that is how the eye works, consciously or unconsciously. There may exist blind musicians and tone-deaf architects but not the reverse. Instead of submitting to the guidance of a so-called objective or naive eye, it would appear to the benefit of architecture to educate and consciously employ the eye, not only for the mechanical transmission of data, but for careful selection of information pertaining to a work's formal structure.

With respect to the application of formal structure, we observed earlier, particularly in the comparisons of Schinkel's Altes Museum with Johnson's Sheldon Art Gallery and Jefferson's University of Virginia campus with Barnes's Purchase campus, how one set of buildings—Schinkel's and Jefferson's—call on the eyes to lead the intellect and the emotions to a richer understanding of the architecture, subtly revealing a true symbiosis between appearance and purpose; while the other set of buildings—Johnson's and

Barnes's—permit, by less controlled and more literal appeal to the eyes, only a discontinuous grasp of the building, as if its attributes were presented by flash cards.

Gropius's fundamental misconception about the nature of perception has, or implies, psychological, aesthetic, and ultimately cultural corollaries. All of them, I am convinced, relate in some way to the genesis and existence of the Bauhaus-legacy buildings, those discussed here and other, less known ones. A few of the corollaries we have touched upon; others now emerge.

First, in the service of pragmatic aesthetics, is the mechanistic treatment of visual phenomena. This leads to a preoccupation with measurable optical effects such as optical illusions and, by extension, tactile and pseudotactile effects. In "Blueprint of an Architect's Education" Gropius proclaims:

We are able today to feed the creative *instinct* [italics mine] of a designer with richer knowledge of visual facts, such as the phenomena of optical illusion, of the relation of solids and voids in space, of light and shade, of color and of scale; objective facts instead of arbitrary, subjective interpretation or formulas long since stale.[46]

It goes without saying that metaphorical, symbolic, and perhaps abstract formal qualities of an object, let alone a space, would not be considered "objective facts" and thus would not be considered visual characteristics.

The second corollary is the surely unintentional impoverishment of architecture as a carrier of cultural meaning through the promotion of pseudotactile qualities which appeal to the most rudimentary, least conscious aesthetic sensibilities and encourage a hopelessly romantic sort of neo-primitivism. On the whole, that encouragement, as we have seen in discussing the Harvard curriculum, is quite deliberate, though, in my opinion, deleterious to a historical understanding of, and therefore intelligent participation in, our culture.

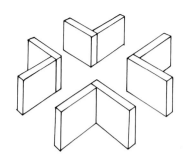

118
Froebel games. After G. C. Manson, *Frank Lloyd Wright to 1910*, Reinhold, New York, 1958.

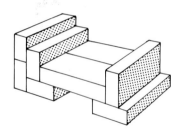

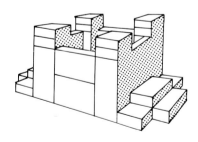

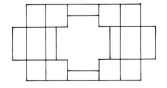

119
Le Corbusier. Anatomical
drawings of nature,
1903.

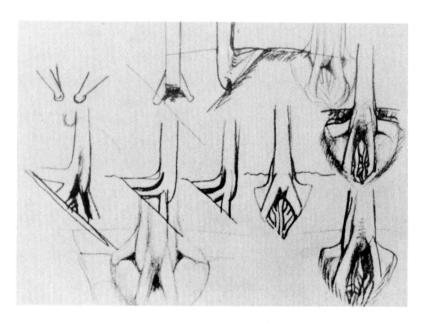

Third among the corollaries, implying great na-ïveté with respect to the nature of forms, is the belief that forms are neutral carriers of meaning. They supposedly express what you want them to express for whatever reasons. This applies primarily to the treatment of a building's appearance. Conversely, and often simultaneously, forms are taken to be the simple, uncontrolled by-products of pragmatic, that is, scientific, design operations. The plan of a Bauhaus-legacy building is often rationalized in this way unless its form has been subjected to the first mode of treatment.

In considering neutral as against archetypal form, a look at the training of Frank Lloyd Wright and Le Corbusier—two great contemporaries of Walter Gropius—may prove instructive. In contrast to the Bauhaus education, Wright's early teaching (fig. 118), the Froebel games to which he was introduced by his mother, and Le Corbusier's equivalent experiences (fig. 119), inspired by his art-school drawing teacher, L'Eplattenier, explored form systematically as a carrier of meaning about itself, nature, and the manmade world. Both the Froebel and L'Eplattenier methods stressed the logic of form generation, be it by invention or by observing nature. Even though Froebel's exercises were less nature-derived than L'Eplattenier's, both saw any given form as a stage in a potential (Froebel) or literal (L'Eplattenier) transformation sequence, in itself a highly useful generalization. Bauhaus training reduced the pleasure principle to an end in itself, while Froebel and L'Eplattenier employed it only in order to interest the student in learning form principles. While the first stressed tactile and pseudotactile pleasures, the last two aimed at the intellectual pleasure of investing forms with meaning derived from cumulative experience.

Not only does the eye select and then record while the camera only records, but the eye, in the process of designing, can instigate thought, as is powerfully demonstrated by Alvar Aalto's beginning sketches for Villa Mairea (fig. 120). On the same piece of paper appear the rudiments of the upper floor plan and a perspective of the building's most prominent corner as seen by an approaching visitor. Apparently the designer has made decisions about priorities: in both drawing versions the "lesser" aspects are barely marked, while the site and the disposition of master/mistress suite are essentially formed. There is no question of divorcing plan from appearance. The building is clearly thought of as an entity at once rational and emotional.

The fourth and last corollary of Gropius's misunderstanding of perception is confusion between subjective and objective values in one's own design work. It is embodied in the tendency of the Bauhaus-inspired curriculum to discourage self-awareness on the part of the designer. The design process being taken to be objective, there is naturally little motivation for personal engagement on the conceptual level. But without articulated self-awareness there can be no self-criticism, a requisite of any creative process that is not to resort to such utterly subjective short-circuit judgments as "what I like is good" and "what feels good is good."

On the architectural level, something rather curious happens when such subjectivity is combined with its polar opposite, the attitude implied by "the plan calculates itself," as apparently happens with so many Bauhaus-legacy buildings. A subjective/objective seesaw forms (see table on p. 97), which becomes the vehicle for escape from criticism. On the one side is the inalienable democratic right to self-expression, while on the other is the inevitable result of scientific operations. The combination is so powerful as to have succeeded to this day in protecting most Bauhaus-legacy and particularly Harvard/Gropius architecture from more than cursory criticism.

The obvious concluding question is what to do about all of those supposedly negative influences. One course of action suggests itself for

120
Alvar Aalto. Villa Mairea, Noormarkku, Finland, 1936, early sketches of upper floor plan and most prominent view.

the architecture school studio: the nature and role of "creative instinct," as Gropius put it, has to be included in the pedagogical discourse rather than relegated to the realm of ineffable mystique. In other words, a certain degree of self-consciousness is to be welcomed and nurtured by, among other means, a critical study of history of forms, spaces, and objects which are to be imbued with meaning that reaches all levels of human endeavor, the mundane as well as the esoteric. The aim ought to be to make architecture, through a rational design discourse (literally and figuratively speaking), into a major resource for the intellectual and emotional enrichment of everyone's life, instead of an endless parade of supposedly pragmatic solutions providing meaningless optical excitement and forever portraying the same tiresome confusion of objective and subjective values. We have seen how important Bauhaus teaching, as well as the personalities of its chief teachers, have been to the buildings it produced. Perhaps the conscious employment of rational discourse can help to clarify some of the recurring confusions and myths and to overcome the inherited liabilities of the Bauhaus-inspired curriculum—the architecture produced under its tutelage or in blind reaction against it.

Every new generation of architectural practitioners, critics, and educators reacts to the context it finds itself in with a matching program. Walter Gropius, principally through the Bauhaus and the Graduate School of Design at Harvard, reacted against what he perceived to be the pernicious values of an intellectual, bookish, and egotistical architecture by crusading for the teaching and practice of a pragmatic, tectonically oriented, and team-produced architecture. Most of his students at Harvard, in turn, renounced their teacher's more explicit exhortations by opening offices in their own names where they could indulge in the production of artistic masterpieces. Yet, since all human experience is cumulative, a person's schooling remains part of his life and work. We are all in some sense graduates of our formative philosophies. And, inevitably, the call for a more highly self-conscious, urbanistically responsive, and intellectually engaging architecture, is meant, at least in part, as the beginning of a program of teaching and practice born out of reaction to the Bauhaus legacy.

ICONOGRAPHIC IMPLICATIONS OF SOME FORMAL CHARACTERISTICS

The Building as an Expression of Institutional Authority		The Building as an Expression of Democratic Laisser Aller	
Characteristics	Consequences	Consequences	Characteristics
Plan			*Plan*
Tendency to force functional relationship diagram into a preconceived form	Totem-like power play of forms	The built diagram	Tendency to express functional relationships
Plan & Appearance			*Plan & Appearance*
Tendency to underarticulate	Overscaling: objects appear larger than they are, i.e., as monuments	Underscaling: objects appear smaller than they are, i.e., as "houses or villages"	Tendency to overarticulate
	Unitary ensemble at the expense of part articulation	Part articulation at the expense of unitary ensemble	
Preference for symmetry	Overall order tends to be dogmatic or banal	Overall order tends to be ad hoc and difficult to comprehend	Avoidance of symmetry
Easily identifiable, diagrammatic hierarchy of parts	Entry obvious to the point of excessive symbolism	Entry difficult to identify	Avoidance of hierarchy
Appearance			*Appearance*
Preference for smooth, uninterrupted surfaces (cast-in-place concrete; facing in polished stone, glass or sintered brick, etc.)	Emphasis on monumentality of scale by absence of surface cues	Emphasis on domesticity of scale by redundancy of surface cues	Preference for alternating rough and smooth surfaces (textured concrete; agglomeration of many different materials and textures)
	Ensemble of volumes and forms tends to dominate surface textures and choice of materials	Surface textures and choice of materials tend to dominate ensemble of volumes and forms	
	Result: The totem without meaning	Result: The decorated diagram	

4 BUILDINGS AND CONVICTIONS

The obvious response to an exegesis such as this is: What of it, what now? The reader has been encouraged to take a good, possibly a first, look at architecture that has been produced—perhaps not entirely consciously—under the influence of Walter Gropius's beliefs and force of personality and that of his younger ally Marcel Breuer by what turned out to be their most prominent students at the Graduate School of Design at Harvard. In the course of contrasting or confronting the ethos of their teaching as promised and portrayed in school bulletins and available studio problems with examples of built architecture, a number of fundamental design principles have been demonstrated, collected under the concept of formal structure.

If one accepts the notion that any teaching of architecture presupposes a certain set of beliefs and that such beliefs more often than not find their manifestation in the works produced by its graduates, then the way architecture is taught becomes quite important. It would thus appear self-evident that the quality of education an architect has received carries beyond the specific building commission to architecture in general. Under the rubric of architecture in general there now exists a curious paradox, developed in recent times and growing more acute all the time: that most current buildings designed in the name of cultural continuity—in emulation or reaction to such gospels as vernacularism, the ideology and methodology of bricolage, neorationalism, and a gaggle of other seductive ideas tethered together under postmodernism—are more likely to weaken and fracture that continuity than to strengthen it. At the same time, yet another persuasion, high tech, can be regarded as an emulating mutation of the modern movement itself. And *all* purport to bear the same Good News: architecture is a vital force in our daily lives—a message hardly to be disputed.

Now, in the face of this diverse array, and given the commonly recognized confusion of meaning and purpose in architecture, it seems quite natural to want to find and emphasize those aspects of architecture which endure, those which most unequivocally represent human behavior and expectations. For architecture, form in its most primary state is the fundamental analog to human behavior and expectations, transcending all boundaries among the many persuasions now before us and offering the best means of unifying them. Further, without a strong recognition in both teaching and practice of the intrinsic implications of forms and the spaces they delineate, throughout the whole range of architectural concerns, even the most ardent wish to imbue a building with symbolic meaning—a characteristic particularly evident in today's polemicizing architecture—comes to naught.

The intention of this essay, in the service of the primacy of form and space in architecture, has been to establish that visual truths are equal to verbal and written truths, to clarify some "old" mid-twentieth-century confusions about what architecture ought to be, and to encourage a sharper, more independent, and certainly more critical eye for future encounters with architecture.

APPENDIXES

Appendix A comprises three student problems given in Gropius's master's class (called Architecture 2d in the GSD bulletin) from the period 1948–1951. Since there are no student problems in the GSD archives dating from before 1947 (save a small landscaping problem from 1946), none of Breuer's bachelor's studio problem formulations are available. (He retired from teaching in 1946.) Thus the master of architecture degree program is better represented in my discussion than the bachelor of architecture program. It is hard to believe, though remotely possible, that the two programs would have differed widely in content, formulation, or intent. Perhaps if all the relevant material becomes accessible it will be possible to study this potential disparity. In the meantime (and most likely even after such a study), Walter Gropius's problem formulations can be considered a fair indication of the values that characterized those heady years.

Appendix B reproduces the 1946–1947 GSD bulletin in excerpted form. From 1938–1939 to the end of Gropius's tenure in 1953 the tone and the essential content of the bulletin remained similar from year to year, with occasional alterations in sequence and subject matter of the school description and once in a while a course. The bulletin published in 1935–1936—just before Gropius's arrival—begins with a brief history of the school followed by a description of the professional prospects awaiting a newly graduated architect, whereas the bulletin of 1938–1939 begins with an anouncement that courses in the history of architecture, formerly part of the GSD curriculum, are henceforth to be taught by Harvard College. This is followed by a brief history of the Graduate School of Design from which any reference to the fine arts has disappeared (in previous bulletins architecture was treated as a subcategory of fine arts). By 1945 the history of the school has been relegated to "General Information" in the last section of the bulletin, to stay there through the Gropius era—and beyond. The implication is that the teaching of architecture at the GSD took a radical turn with Gropius's arrival; school continuity and a sense of tradition were no longer wanted.

The course requirements and descriptions as presented in the 1946–1947 bulletin (Appendix B) differ very little in substance from those in the 1938–1939 bulletin, and those appearing after 1947 through 1953 differ not at all. Hence the 1946–1947 bulletin seems to be representative of the school's general intentions.

A: Three Student Problem Formulations
by Walter Gropius

A1

Arch. 2d   HARVARD UNIVERSITY - GSD   Issued: 9/26 51
  Walter Gropius   Due: 10/8/51
  William Lyman   Sketch Problem   2:00 PM

_____

A Site Development for Family Residences

One of the great tasks facing today's architects, and especially in the
field of housing, is the problem of reconciling the economic advantages of
mass production of standardized building parts with man's desire for
individuality. The tendency is toward greater standardization of building
parts in an attempt to offset ever-increasing building costs. At the
same time - and for the same reason - housing accomodations and the
land area they occupy have grown smaller. The inevitable results, where
those economic pressures have been allowed to govern, are communities
like Leavittown, where man's individuality finds expression in a different coat of paint.

The overemphasis on being different from one's neighbor instead of on the
search for a common denominator in architecture characterized the flight
of the last generation of architects from the presumed anti-human influence
of the machine. Confusing cause and effect, they made a futile attempt
to swim against the stream thus frustrating the achievement of a superior
architectural beauty which would become apparent in neighborhood units
designed to be a harmonized entity. Now it has become a major task of
the architect to promote the use of the machine for the process of building
as this implies increasing economic advantages and, at the same time, to
develop flexible means of design which would soften the regimentation
and starkness of repetitive machine production.

Perhaps the most significant attempt to reduce the cost of housing has
been through prefabrication. On the one hand, there was the Lustron
type of approach - to produce houses like automobiles.Those who
recognized the need for respecting man's individuality held little
enthusiasm for such undertakings, dooming them before they started. On
the other hand, several attempts have been made to develop systems of
flexible prefabricated building parts which could be used inter-
changeably to produce the diversity of appearance which man demands.
Future success in prefabrication hinges upon the issue of making those
opposites meet. Or, as Frank Lloyd Wright once put it, "standardization
can be murder or beneficial factor as the life in the thing standardized is kept by imagination or destroyed be the lack of it"

Prefabrication alone, no matter how rapidly it may succeed, will be
but a partial answer to the problem of providing satisfactory housing
at prices most people can afford. Houses will continue to be built
by conventional methods for many years to come. Various stages of
prefabrication will be utilized where particular situations make them
possible, such as plumbing assemblies, pre-cut lumber, roof trusses, etc.

But in order even to take advantage of these limited economics, certain amount of standardization of floor plans will be necessary. From this it would seem (and most current subdivisions prove it) that one of the contributions architects could make at this moment would be to investigate the various ways of arranging semi-standarized plans on the land. This investigation will be the subject of this problem.

The student is asked to select a 3-bedroom house of his liking, one he has designed or a plan by another, and on the site chosen explore the possibilities of achieving visual variety by such means as the following:

a. Use alternately the plan as well as its mirror.
b. Place the house at different angles to the sun.
c. Alternate the materials, their textures and colors, and alternate the bright and dark effect.
d. Confine the adjacent outdoor living space around the house by varying combinations of pergolas, trellis, screens hedges, fences, shrubs, and groups of trees.
e. Place the garage or car port at different angles to the house.
f. Add a screen porch to the house in different positions and angles.

To a large degree this means thinking creatively more about the spaces outside the house than those inside. The blunt extreme, where seemingly the former are never thought about, is the average speculative development which in growing numbers obliterate the American landscape.

Requirements:

1. Plot plan with roadway and access roads, showing the location of the houses and accessories and the landscaping. Scale to be determined later.

2. Make a series of perspective sketches showing the varieties of appearences in spite of using the same house type.

Architecture 2d	HARVARD UNIVERSITY – GSD	Issued : 11/2/48
Mr. Gropius		Due : 2/2/49
Mr. Peabody		Jury : 2/3/49
Mr. Lyman	Problem II	

AN ELEMENTARY SCHOOL FOR OAK HILL PARK, NEWTON, MASSACHUSETTS

> " A rule is so easy that it does not need a man to apply it;
> an automaton, a machine, can be made to keep a school so.
> It facilitates labor and thought so much that there is always
> the temptation in large schools to omit the endless task of
> meeting the wants of each single mind, and to govern by steam.
> But it is at a frightful cost.Our modes of Education aim to
> expedite, to save labor; to do for masses what cannot be done
> for masses, what must be done reverently, one by one! say
> rather, the whole world is needed for the tuition of each
> pupil. . . . . or we sacrifice the genius of the pupil, the
> unknown possibilities of his nature, to a neat and safe uniformity,
> as the Turks whitewash the costly mosaics of ancient art which
> the Greeks left on their temple walls. Rather let us have men
> whose manhood is only the continuation of their boyhood, natural
> characters still; such are able and fertile for heroic action;
> and not that sad spectacle with which we are too familiar,
> educated eyes in uneducated bodies."
>
> Emerson

The subject of this problem is the design of an elementary school for Oak Park Hill,
a development of 412 single family units nearing completion in the southern section
of the City of Newton. Planned and built by the city and its Veterans' Housing
Department, the development will contain its own shopping area in addition to
the School. The homes are to be sold for about $8,000 (without garage). All land
and land improvement costs are borne by the City.

The City of Newton is recognized as having one of the best public school systems
in the nation and consequently it goes without saying that the decision to erect
the Oak Hill Park School came not merely as a result of the sudden building of
400 new homes but rather was based on a long range school development program in which
the Oak Hills Park School is but one part of an integrated whole. How this particular project is integrated with Newton's overall school needs will be explained
with slides early in the problem.

Inasmuch as the school will be the only cultural and recreational facility within
the development, it must be designed as much to serve the needs of the parents as
those of their children. This dual function becomes more apparent when one stops
to consider that even in communities considered to be below standard as to provision
of cultural and recreational facilities, a wider variety of the latter is usually
provided than will be the case here. This somewhat disturbing fact – that over 400
families will have to depend on one facility for their "in-close" cultural and
recreational needs – demands the fullest utilization of the site, in terms both of
actual program and flexibility of spaces. The site itself is a flat, four-sided
plot of 4.7 acres, located somewhat off the center of population of the development.

Classroom size recommended by the Newton School Committee is based not on so many
square feet per pupil but on what is considered to be the optimum functional
classroom unit. Translated in terms of square feet this unit results in the provision
of approximately 30 feet per pupil. A requirement of the present program calls for
provision for future expansion of the number of classrooms by about 40%. A small
percentage, possibly 10-15%, of the children attending the school will live
outside the development. Although they will be within walking distance of the
school, some provision should be made for arrival by motor vehicle during
inclement waeather.

Architecture 2d   HARVARD UNIVERSITY — GSD   Issued: April 5, 1948
   Professor Gropius   Due: June 2, 1948
   Mr. Lyman   Problem IV   (10:00AM)

A GRADUATE CENTER FOR HARVARD UNIVERSITY

General:

Harvard University plans to build on Jarvis Field a "Graduate Center" consisting of a central kitchen and dining halls equipped to serve approximately
1,000 students and containing in addition one large asembly room and several
smaller common rooms, lounging or meeting rooms; and new dormitories to accommodate approximately 700 students.

The overall program will consist of three individual projects separately fin-
anced by three distinct departments of the University working in cooperation.
While from the design standpoint the project must be conceived as a whole, the
specific requirements of the three participating groups must be considered individually and the costs must be kept within the stated financial resources of
the three respective departments.

The three individual projects and the departments concerned are as follows:

A. The University plans to contribute Jarvis Field as the site for the three
projects, cleared for construction; and will thereon construct the building
containing the kitchen, dining hall, large meeting room, and miscellaneous
smaller meeting rooms including the furnishings of all room. Included also
will be the running of necessary utilities, grading, landscaping, and building
of roads and walks.

B. The Law School contemplates construction of one or more dormitories which,
together with exising Hastings Hall, will house approximately 500 students.
As Hastings Hall now accommodates 113 students, plus proctors, the new construction should accommodate roughly 400 students.

C. The Graduate School of Arts and Sciences, in participation with graduate
and professional schools other than the Law School, contemplates the construction of one or more dormitories which together with existing Conant,
Perkins and Divinity Halls will house approximately 500 students. As these
three halls now accommodate 295 students, plus proctors, the new construction
should accommodate roughly 210 students.

Our attention in this problem will be directed mainly at finding the best
accommodations, as to livability and flexibility, that can be obtained within
the budget available The final solution to the problem must, therefore, be
based on finding a balance between the relatively rigid requirements of economy and construction, and the less definable psychological requirements which,
when met, provide a stimulating environment for education. In the search for
a solution the student must not only keep in mind the utmost economy in construction compatible with requirements, but also utmost economy in operation
so as to enable the rent charged the students to be as low as possible. It
is hoped that said rents will be considerable lower than those paid by studnets
housed in the Houses and Yard dormitories. One phase of this problem, therefore, is to arrive at the type of construction involving the minimum operating
expense for heating, lighting and cleaning. The possiblity of maximum mechanization of these operations must be thoroughly explored.

Arch. 2d - Prob. IV - 1948

Work Program:

The emphasis within this problem will naturally be on research into all the factors bearing on design, construction and economy, in the conduct of which the class will be assisted by the University representatives of the student body.

The University departments involved in this project have already undertaken to arrive at decisions concerning sizes of dormitory rooms, and toward that end the Building and Grounds Department has set up in the Biological Building mock-ups of typical single and double rooms. At such time as the class has reached preliminary conslusions as to the design of dormitory rooms, the Building and Grounds Department will provide materials and manpower assistance to enable these rooms to be constructed by the class complete with rough built-in furniture.

It is further intended that student committees from the graduate schools involved will be asked to view the rooms thus constructed and to discuss with the class the advantages and disadvantages of the various arrangements.

It would seem advisible that the class appoint one member of the class to coordinate the numerous fields of research which this problem entails, and that working with and responsible to him would be research "captains" heading up each of the research teams.

Two purposes, insofar as the University is concerned, should be kept in mind for the presentation. First, although it may not prove difficult to gain visual acceptance by the University of designs as developed by the class, the hard fact remains that the final decisions may hinge largely on dollars and cents. For that reason it is imperative that every avenue of economy be explored and that the final presentation take into full account the importance of the economic phase of the research.

Second, it is currently the intention of the University to make use of the findings and drawings in the literature they will have to prepare for the raising of funds to finance the project.

Supplemental Information:

A. Dining Hall, Kitchen and Meeting Rooms. At present the University has in mind a layout similar to Cowie Hall, the present dining hall for the Business School, but of first-class construction. Part of this problem will be to investigate thoroughly the operation of Cowie Hall as the basis for a more thorough study of the whole problem of dining halls and their integration with the additonal student facilities called for in this project. An influencing factor in this connection will be the relative views of the sponsors of the two dormitory projects, as yet not expressed, as to the desirability of single versus separate dining halls for the students of their respective schools.

It is tentatively suggested that the large meeting room be of at least the square foot area of the common room in Kirkland House, the largest house available, and preferably larger. Probably even more imporant than the relationship of this room to the dining room(s) is that of the smaller lounges and meeting rooms, inasmuch as one of their main functions is to enable the students of the various schools to mingle readily with one another.

Arch. 2d - Prob. IV - 1948

B. Law School Dormitories. When this project was first submitted to the Corporation, the Building and Grounds Department submitted schematic plans of the
simplest type of dormitory unit which it estimated could be constructed for
$2,691 per student plus $211 per student for standard dormitory furniture, or
a total cost of just over $2,900 per student. As it was then felt that the
facilities proposed were possibly too spartan and might be considered too un-
attractive in comparison with existing dormitories, it was decided that more
leeway ought to be provided. To this end, in addition to increasing the room
areas, it is contemplated that a minimum of one common room will be provided
in each dormitory, possibly in the basement. This "addition" is reflected in
the cost estimates. Approximately $100,000 of the $1,500,000 which the Law
School hopes to raise for this project will be used for modernization and redecoration of Hastings Hall.

C. Graduate School Dormitories. Inasmuch as the graduate and professional
schools involved in this part (C) of the overall project may have difficulty in
raising as much money proportionately as the Law School, it may be necessary to
provide quarters for these students at a correspondingly lower cost per student
although the University authorities would prefer not to make any distinction
between schools as to quality of accommodations. The difficulty in avoiding
this distinction is increased by the fact that this project (C) involves in
addition to new construction, the modernization and redecoration of three
existing dormitories as compred to one in the case of the Law School

D.. Single Versus Double Rooms. As to the questions of ratio of single to double rooms, the present attitude of the University department heads involved appears to be that equal numbers of each are desireable. However, there is ample
evidence that a solution consisting wholly of double rooms would be acceptable
if the proper design of such a room can be found and if the student committees
show a preference for this type of room. The advantage in economy, both in
construction and operation, are obvious. This question will be discussed
further in class.

B: Bulletin, Graduate School of Design,
Harvard University, 1946–1947 (Excerpts)

THE GRADUATE SCHOOL
OF DESIGN

Courses in Architecture
Landscape Architecture
City and Regional Planning

[1946–1947]

CAMBRIDGE, MASSACHUSETTS
PUBLISHED BY THE UNIVERSITY

THE FACULTY OF DESIGN

JAMES BRYANT CONANT, PH.D., LL.D., S.D., L.H.D., D.C.L., D.S.C., President of the University.

JOSEPH HUDNUT, B.ARCH., S.M., A.M., Professor of Architecture and Dean of the Faculty of Design.

CHARLES WILSON KILLAM, Professor of Architecture, Emeritus.

HENRY VINCENT HUBBARD, S.B., A.M., Charles Dyer Norton Professor of Regional Planning, Emeritus.

JOHN SANFORD HUMPHREYS, Professor of Architecture, Emeritus.

WALTER GROPIUS, A.M., SC.D., Professor of Architecture and Chairman of the Department of Architecture.

BREMER WHIDDEN POND, S.B., M.L.A., Charles Eliot Professor of Landscape Architecture and Chairman of the Department of Landscape Architecture.

GEORGE HOLMES PERKINS, A.B., M.ARCH., Charles Dyer Norton Professor of Regional Planning and Chairman of the Department of Regional Planning.

KENNETH JOHN CONANT, M.ARCH., PH.D., LITT.D., Professor of Architecture.

HENRY ATHERTON FROST, A.B., M.ARCH., Professor of Architecture and Chairman of the Department of Architectural Sciences.

WALTER FRANCIS BOGNER, Professor of Architecture.

*MARCEL BREUER, Associate Professor of Architecture.

MARTIN WAGNER, DR.ING., Associate Professor of Regional Planning.

JEAN-GEORGES PETER, S.B., S.M. IN C.E., Associate Professor of Architecture.

WALTER LOUIS CHAMBERS, B.L.A., M.L.A., Associate Professor of Landscape Architecture.

HUGH ASHER STUBBINS, JR., S.B. IN ARCH., M.ARCH., Associate Professor of Architecture.

STEPHEN FRANCIS HAMBLIN, S.B., Assistant Professor of Horticulture.

NORMAN THOMAS NEWTON, S.B., M.L.D., Assistant Professor of Landscape Architecture.

* On leave of absence.

GRADUATE SCHOOL OF DESIGN

EDWARD KEENE TRUE, S.B. IN A.E., Assistant Professor of Architecture.

GEORGE TYRRELL LeBOUTILLIER, Assistant Professor of Design.

CHARLES HENRY BURCHARD, M.ARCH., Assistant Professor of Architecture.

EDWARD LOUIS ULLMAN, S.B., A.M., PH.D., Assistant Professor of Regional Planning.

LEONARD JAMES CURRIE, B.ARCH., M.ARCH., Assistant Professor of Architecture.

LESTER ALBERTSON COLLINS, A.B., M.L.A., Instructor in Landscape Architecture.

CATHERINE BAUER, A.M., Lecturer on Housing.

WILLIAM LINDUS CODY WHEATON, A.B., Lecturer on Regional Planning.

MAHLON GILMAN KNOWLES, S.B. IN M.E., Lecturer on the Mechanical Equipment of Buildings.

JOHN CHEESMAN HARKNESS, A.B., B.ARCH., M.ARCH., Assistant in Architecture.

RUTH V. COOK, Librarian of the Department of Architecture.

KATHERINE McNAMARA, Librarian of the Department of Landscape Architecture and Regional Planning.

SALLY SYMONDS RAABE, Secretary of the School of Design.

COUNCIL OF THE DEPARTMENT OF REGIONAL PLANNING

GEORGE HOLMES PERKINS, A.B., M.ARCH., Charles Dyer Norton Professor of Regional Planning and Chairman of the Department of Regional Planning.

WALTER GROPIUS, A.M., DR.ING., Professor of Architecture and Chairman of the Department of Architecture.

MARTIN WAGNER, DR.ING., Associate Professor of Regional Planning.

MORRIS BRYAN LAMBIE, PH.D., L.H.D., Professor of Government, Graduate School of Public Administration.

JOSEPH HUDNUT, B.ARCH., S.M., A.M., Professor of Architecture and Dean of the Faculty of Design.

DERWENT STAINTHORPE WHITTLESEY, PH.D., Professor of Geography.

[4]

THE FACULTY OF DESIGN

Carl Joachim Friedrich, dr.phil., Professor of Government, Graduate School of Public Administration.

Seymour Edwin Harris, a.b., ph.d., Associate Professor of Economics, Graduate School of Public Administration.

Talcott Parsons, a.b., ph.d., Professor of Sociology and Chairman of the Department of Sociology.

Charles Cortez Abbott, ph.d., Associate Professor of Business Economics, Graduate School of Business Administration.

VISITING COMMITTEE OF THE SCHOOL OF DESIGN

Jerome D. Greene, a.m., ll.d., *Chairman.*

Charles S. Ascher, ll.b., *City Planner.*

Robert P. Bellows, Diplomé Ecole des Beaux Arts, *Architect.*

Arthur F. Brinckerhoff, b.s.a., *Landscape Architect.*

George Howe, Diplomé Ecole des Beaux Arts, *Architect.*

Niels H. Larsen, *Architect.*

Charles D. Maginnis, ll.d., *Architect.*

Charles E. Merriam, ll.d., *Professor of Political Science,* University of Chicago.

Robert B. Mitchell, s.b. in arch., *City Planner.*

Eliel Saarinen, ph.d., dr.arch., and c.p., d.eng., art.d., *Architect.*

Henry R. Shepley, Diplomé Ecole des Beaux Arts, *Architect.*

Otto J. Teegen, m.arch., *Architect.*

Edward C. Whiting, a.b., *Landscape Architect.*

Bradford Williams, m.l.a., *Landscape Architect.*

[5]

Foreword

The purpose of this pamphlet is to offer to prospective students and to others who may be interested an account of the professional curricula in architecture, landscape architecture and city and regional planning at Harvard University.

This account is given in three parts.

Part One (pages 7 to 26) includes descriptions of the programs of professional studies in each field together with the requirements for admission and the conditions governing the recommendations for degrees.

Part Two (pages 26 to 38) includes detailed descriptions of the courses which form elements in the programs of study described in Part One.

Part Three (pages 38 to 50) includes general information in respect to the School of Design: a brief history of the School, a description of its buildings and equipment, data relating to fees, expenses, scholarships, and the rules governing registration.

PART ONE

THE PROGRAMS OF PROFESSIONAL STUDIES

The Graduate School of Design offers three programs of study leading to Bachelor's degrees in architecture, landscape architecture or city planning. In addition, programs of advanced study leading to the Master's degree in architecture, landscape architecture, city planning or regional planning are offered.

The programs of study are intended as introductions to these professions. They include the knowledge and techniques which, when supplemented by practical experience, form the basic equipment in these professions; and they afford also an organized and progressive discipline in those habits of thought and of vision which are essential to successful practice.

The Requirements for Admission

To be admitted to the School of Design as a candidate for a professional degree a student must normally have completed satisfactorily and in an approved college a course of study leading to the degree *Bachelor of Arts* or *Bachelor of Science*. There are, however, several exceptions to this rule. These are:

(a) Returning members of the armed forces who have completed satisfactorily two years in an approved college may be admitted as candidates for the Bachelor's degree.

(b) Graduates of approved schools of architecture and landscape architecture may be admitted for graduate study and, under the conditions noted on pages 17 and 20 respectively, such graduates will be accepted as candidates for the Master's degree in architecture or landscape architecture.

(c) Graduates of approved schools of architecture and landscape architecture may be admitted to candidacy, with

[7]

advanced standing, for the Bachelor's degree in city planning.

(d) Graduates of approved colleges who have been awarded a Master's degree in the social or political sciences, in architecture or in landscape architecture may be admitted to candidacy for the Master's degree in city or regional planning. Such candidates must have had not less than one year's professional experience in a planning agency.

Students who expect to enter one of the Departments in the School of Design should write to the Secretary of that Department, Robinson Hall, Cambridge 38, Massachusetts, for one of the forms used in applying for admission. This form should be filled out and returned to the Secretary together with a transcript of the applicant's record in college not later than one month before the registration day of an academic term. (The dates of registration are given in the academic calendar published each year. See p. 38.)

Students who have completed in another school any part of a curriculum (or its equivalent) offered in the School of Design may apply for advanced standing when applying for admission.

Special students (not candidates for a degree) are seldom admitted, but the Dean will consider in exceptional cases applications for admission on this basis.

Preparation in College

Architecture, landscape architecture and city planning are professions which require for success special aptitudes, arduous techniques and a sustained experience of practice; but they require also for any distinguished achievement wide knowledge and social insight. They are technical services but they are also arts of expression having as their theme some imprint of the human spirit upon its environment. Technical service well rendered is an essential of modern civilization and is rightly a source of satisfaction to its practitioners; but the student who takes up the study of architecture, landscape

[8]

architecture or city planning should understand that the deeper and enduring rewards and the wider usefulness which these may afford are inaccessible to men whose technical competence is unsustained by wide cultural interests.

A college is by no means the only theatre for spiritual and intellectual growth; but it is one which is established, available and consciously directed towards that end. A college training does not comprise merely courses of instruction; it comprises, rather, a pattern of life continued for a period of years in an environment peculiarly adapted for the development of the mind and spirit. College life includes, besides instruction and the experiences of laboratory and classroom, participation in a unique social and intellectual world, association with men of like sympathies and ambitions and, above all, freedom to discover values and means.

College life is not inconsistent (as some suppose) with vocational preparation. College students who expect at a later time to take up the professional study of architecture, landscape architecture or planning should select their courses of study and plan their extra-curricular activities in such a way as to make these a foundation on which they may build. The Dean of the School of Design will gladly advise such students, all of whom are invited to bring their problems to his attention.

College students who expect to take up the study of architecture or landscape architecture should include in their college curriculum courses in the physical sciences. For architects, courses in physics and in mathematics are recommended; for landscape architects, courses in chemistry, geology, mathematics and biology; and for planners, economics, sociology, government and contemporary history. These courses should be, so far as is practicable, experimental courses: that is to say, courses so conducted as to require a direct experience with subject matter. Lecture courses are less valuable to students of design than courses in which they may observe and evaluate their own experiences and reflections.

[9]

The Faculty of Design does not recommend courses for their "disciplinary value"; but it is obvious that men who expect to design buildings must learn to command such tools as mathematics and mechanics. These are also of unquestionable value as elements in a wide survey of human life; a survey which should include the study of English literature, or philosophy when this is addressed to problems in the conduct of life, of a foreign language and especially the study of the arts of music, painting and architecture.

Whenever it is practicable college students should take courses in the theory and practice of design. They will find especially valuable those courses in which making and doing, rather than learning, are the essential methods: shop courses and studio courses, in which idea and concept are translated into visible patterns. Drawing, painting, sculpture and craft work should be practised continuously; and where such experiences are not afforded within a college curriculum, the college student should seek them in extra-curricular activities.

Harvard College and Radcliffe College

To assist students who expect to study architecture, landscape architecture and city planning, Harvard College and Radcliffe College have established special departments called *Departments of Architectural Sciences*. A department is, in effect, a committee of the Faculty having charge of a definite field of instruction. Under the rules of both colleges students may choose *architectural sciences* as their field of concentration and receive throughout their college years the advice and guidance of the Department of Architectural Sciences which includes several instructors who are also members of the Faculty of Design. The Department publishes a special pamphlet which gives the rules and procedures for concentration in *architectural sciences* and which gives also descriptive outlines of special courses open to students in this field. Typical

[10]

THE PROGRAMS OF PROFESSIONAL STUDIES

curricula for students in Harvard and Radcliffe are also included.

Students in Harvard College and in Radcliffe College who elect *architectural sciences* as their field of concentration may take in their final year of college a group of courses which is identical with the group forming the first year of professional study in architecture, landscape architecture or city planning. They may thus include two terms of professional study as a part of their college curriculum and in that way shorten the total length of their academic preparation for practice. Inquiries concerning undergraduate courses in this field should be addressed to the *Chairman of the Department of Architectural Sciences, Hunt Hall, Cambridge 38, Massachusetts.*

Professional Collaboration in the School of Design

There are three departments — architecture, landscape architecture and regional planning — in the School of Design, each of which is in charge of the instruction in its special field.

Each of these fields includes an area of human interest and a technique peculiar to itself and not included in the others; and yet all three are also parts of a common field and have processes and objectives which are and should be identical. Architecture, landscape architecture and city planning are all social arts, inseparable except in rare instances from the collective life, the smallest unit of which is the family; the largest, the population of a city or region. The materials of each art are, if not the same, at least alike in character since they comprise, first, those aspects of human existence which invite structural adaptations and, second, the material substances capable of such adaptations. They are alike also in that they are integral with both the social and physical sciences and attain their vitality and usefulness from that integration.

It is obvious that the instruction in architecture, in landscape architecture and in city and regional planning must gain in breadth and efficiency from an association with the instruc-

[11]

GRADUATE SCHOOL OF DESIGN

tion in these related fields and from the guidance of a common authority. This association in the School of Design is general and sustained. Throughout the curricula of the three Departments there is a continuous relevance to the work of the other Departments. There are frequent and active projects of collaboration and the avenues by which students in one department may participate in the work of the related departments are constantly open.

The First Year in the School of Design

This collaboration is especially evident in the first year of professional study — which, as above noted, may be the final year of study in Harvard College or Radcliffe College. In this first year the program of studies, whether for architects, landscape architects or city planners, is under the direction of a committee representing all three of the Departments.

The objectives of this first-year program are two: first, to acquaint the student with that way of working which is common to the arts of design; and, second, to give him some basic experience with the techniques of the professions associated in this School.

Design in architecture, landscape architecture, and city or regional planning begins with the assembly, correlation and interpretation of social, economic and physical data. From this beginning the designer proceeds to the creation of an imaginative order and to the evolution of an order made up of materials — of shapes, enclosures, structures, surfaces, colors — which conform to the order thus inwardly conceived. Whatever may be its ultimate goal, all education in these arts must be, especially in the preliminary and fundamental phases, addressed to the development of these processes of thought and vision. This must be done not through precept merely or example — still less through the accumulation of factual knowledge — but through such experiences as will establish in the student's mind a clear apprehension of these basic relationships

[12]

and encourage those aptitudes which are specific to this order of creative activity.

These experiences are gradually woven into the study of professional techniques and become inseparable from these. Drawing, graphics and modeling are introduced as means for the communication of ideas: it is here that the student will first meet the demand for originality of concept, economy of means, precise statement and forceful presentation. Considerations specific to the professions follow. These include a study of ground forms and sites, map-reading, topography and simple structures and broad investigations into the patterns of community life. The students are required to visit many properties and to learn at first hand the relation of structure, site and city; they become acquainted, through field trips, graphic representation and the making of models, with the nature of the materials and methods which are basic in their several professions; and these experiences are of course supplemented by theoretical analysis and exercises.

When the student has acquired a sufficient experience with site, shelter and the community, he is given a progressive series of problems in design — problems which include the elements of all three professions. This training in design tends right from its start to develop a habit of integrated thinking in terms of space, technique and economy. The problems are, so far as is practicable, related to actual sites and probable requirements. The procedure is similar to that which obtains in professional practice.

The Program in the First Year

For convenience, the sequence of studies outlined above is organized into three closely integrated courses. The introductory experiences in design and expression are included in *Design I*. These are developed in *Planning I* so as to include the techniques of shelter and site and problems in the design of these, as a result of the student's research into the require-

ments of community life. In *Construction I*, taken concurrently with *Planning I*, the work is supplemented by lectures, discussions, laboratory exercises and field trips; and *Architecture 3* affords the discipline in drawing essential to these studies.

The detailed requirements of these courses and of all other courses will be found in the pages following page 26 under the general heading *Descriptions of Courses*.

Students are advised to begin their course of study in the School at the beginning of the fall term. This is also the beginning of the *academic year*. In special cases students may be permitted by the Dean to register at the beginning of the spring term.

Electives

In each of the professional curricula of the School there are included elective courses which are essential parts of these curricula. The purpose of these electives is to enlarge the range of intellectual interests of the students and to continue throughout the professional course the wider disciplines which were commenced in college.

Students should note that in each of the curricula their choice of electives is limited. In the curriculum leading to the first degree in architecture, for example, the student who has not included among his college studies at least three courses in the history of design must include these among his electives, the selection being made from among those courses which are listed in Part II of this pamphlet (Descriptions of Courses) and marked with an asterisk. Students in architecture, landscape architecture or planning who have not included among their college courses a course in mathematics (through analytic geometry) must make good that deficiency by electing a course in mathematics during their first year in the School.

In the curriculum leading to the first degree in city or regional planning the choice of electives is normally limited to

THE PROGRAMS OF PROFESSIONAL STUDIES

the list prescribed in the curriculum given on pages 23, 24. Students in architecture or landscape architecture must elect at least one course in planning.

The Professional Curricula

After the first year the subject matter and methods in architecture, landscape architecture and city planning become more specifically related to these several fields. Although an active collaboration is continued, each of the three departments assumes an undivided control over the instruction in its field, subject only to the approval of the Faculty as a whole.

The normal period for the completion of the curricula leading to the first professional degrees (B.Arch., B.L.A., B.C.P.) is seven to eight terms – including the first year (two terms) described above; but in no case can the rate of progress of a student be predicted, since this will depend on the quality of his work and not alone upon its quantity. The problem method, initiated in the first year, continues throughout the professional curricula. The student's designs, which include technologies progressively complex, are submitted periodically to juries of the Faculty and these juries have the sole authority to determine the rate of progress for each student. The rules governing the conduct of problems and the awards of juries are published in a leaflet available to all students.

Courses Leading to the Degree Bachelor of Architecture

Problems in the design of buildings form the core of the studies leading to the degree *Bachelor of Architecture*. Buildings are at no time studied without a consideration of site and community, but after the first year the programs for students of architecture are progressively limited to problems having as their important elements useful structures enclosing space. These programs are for convenience arranged in three courses

[15]

GRADUATE SCHOOL OF DESIGN

of study: *Design I, Planning I* (the first year), *Architecture 2b*, and *Architecture 2c*. These form, in effect, one course.

Around this central discipline there are grouped a number of related courses, including courses in the techniques of construction and in professional practice. These are without exception conducted by instructors who are also actively participating in the courses in design so that collaboration is sustained throughout the curriculum. These courses include, besides *Construction I* (given in the first year): *Architecture 4b* and *4d*, architectural engineering; *Architecture 5b*, the mechanical equipment of buildings; and *Architecture 6*, building techniques and professional practice. Descriptions of these courses will be found in the pages following page 29.

All of these courses are related so far as is practicable with the activities of the profession of architecture, so that the relevance of academic study to practice is constantly felt. Field trips, office practice, the study of manufacture and distribution, of costs and accounting; all are essential elements in the curriculum. In addition to this practical experience each student is required at some time before his final year of residence to spend not less than one term in some active field employment directly connected with building operations. This requirement, for convenience, is included in the course *Architecture 4e* described on p. 29.

Besides these professional courses, each student who is a candidate for the degree *Bachelor of Architecture* must pass at the time he is taking *Design I, Planning I*, and *Construction I*, three elective courses, and in each succeeding year two elective courses (two terms). These may be in a related field, including landscape architecture or city planning. No student will be recommended for the degree who has not included among his electives three courses (three terms) in the history of design, unless he has had equivalent courses in another institution.

Upon completion of all the courses required for the degree

[16]

THE PROGRAMS OF PROFESSIONAL STUDIES

Bachelor of Architecture, a student may petition the Chairman of the Department for permission to begin his *thesis*. This is a problem in the design of a building or group of buildings for which the student submits a program. The work must be so formulated and carried out, under the direction and criticism of the Chairman, as to demonstrate the student's ability both in design and the techniques of building construction. This demonstration is the final requirement for the degree.

A typical curriculum leading to the degree *Bachelor of Architecture* follows.

Typical Curriculum in Architecture

The Faculty of Design will recommend for the degree *Bachelor of Architecture* a student who, having satisfied the Faculty in respect to his preparation, has passed with credit the courses listed below:

First Year:	Design I (fall term)
	Planning I (fall and spring terms)
	Construction I (fall and spring terms)
	*Three Electives
Summer Term:	Architecture 4e (at end of either first or second year)
Second Year:	Architecture 2b (fall and spring terms)
	Architecture 4b (fall and spring terms)
	Architecture 4d (end of spring term)
	Architecture 6 (fall and spring terms)
	*Electives (two terms)
Third Year:	Architecture 2c and Thesis (normally three terms)
	Architecture 5b (fall term)
	*Electives (two terms)

The Master's Degree in Architecture

The Department of Architecture offers to graduates of

* The attention of students is directed to the rules governing the choice of electives. See p. 14.

GRADUATE SCHOOL OF DESIGN

approved schools of architecture a course of advanced study (*Architecture 2d*) which combines as parts of a single discipline design, techniques of construction and professional practice. The work in this course is carried on under conditions resembling those in an architect's office but with wider opportunities for creative effort. At least one problem each year is done in collaboration with the Departments of Regional Planning and Landscape Architecture.

The work in *Architecture 2d* consists of major problems of architectural design and planning. These problems will include: (a) the research necessary for the gathering of social and economic data; (b) the detailing of structural elements and of installation; (c) the computation of financing and of operational cost of buildings; and (d) the study of professional practice (specifications, documents, legal problems).

The requirements for the degree *Master in Architecture* include normally the satisfactory completion of *Architecture 2d*; but the Chairman of the Department may require additional work in city planning, construction or mechanical equipment if, in his judgment, a candidate is not sufficiently prepared in these fields. The degree will in no case be granted except after two terms of residence in the School of Design.

Courses Leading to the Degree
Bachelor of Landscape Architecture

Problems in the design of areas of land for human use and enjoyment form, after the first year, the central core of the curriculum in landscape architecture. Landscape architecture — like architecture and city planning — is immediately addressed to the creation of that environment which sustains the life of civilized communities. Its practice demands therefore the same broad disciplines and experience in the solution of practical problems even more diversified than in architecture. These conditions demand an active collaboration with archi-

THE PROGRAMS OF PROFESSIONAL STUDIES

tects, with city and regional planners, and with other professions.

The courses in landscape design required for the degree *Bachelor of Landscape Architecture* and which together form one continuous course are: *Design I, Planning I, Construction I* (given in the first year), *Landscape Architecture 2b,* and *Landscape Architecture 2c*. Interlocking with these are courses in landscape engineering (*Landscape Architecture 4b* and *4c*), in horticulture and plant materials (*Landscape Architecture 6* and *7*), in planting design and professional practice (*Landscape Architecture 8* and *5*), and in graphic representation (*Landscape Architecture 3b* and *3c*). Landscape engineering is that applied science which is concerned with the methods used to modify the surface of the ground and the techniques of such structures — highways, walls, drainage systems and water supply — which are accessory to this science. Horticulture and plant materials are concerned with the plants which form one of the materials of landscape design: their ecological groupings, the operations of planting, the influence of climate and soils. Professional practice includes a basic knowledge of office and field management and the methods involved such as costs, law, relations to clients and to contractors. Graphic representation is especially essential to the landscape architect since he must be able to present his ideas to his client with clarity and conviction and to the contractor with completeness and precision.

Students in landscape architecture must, like students in architecture, include certain elective courses with the approval of the Chairman as indicated in the curriculum in landscape architecture as listed.

Upon completion of all the courses required for the degree *Bachelor of Landscape Architecture*, the candidate for this degree must submit a *thesis* comprising one or more independent designs for landscape projects. The rules governing this thesis may be obtained from the Chairman of the Department.

[19]

PART TWO

DESCRIPTIONS OF COURSES

The courses are grouped under the following headings:

I   Courses offered by the Faculty of Design in the first year required of all candidates for a first degree in architecture, landscape architecture or city planning;

II   Courses offered by the Department of Architecture;

III   Courses offered by the Department of Landscape Architecture;

IV   Courses offered by the Department of Regional Planning.

I

Courses in the first year for all candidates for their first professional degree in architecture, landscape architecture or city planning

DESIGN I. Theory and Practice of Design. *Studio exercises, Tuesday and Thursday, 2–5, and additional hours.* Fall term. Assistant Professor LEBOUTILLIER, with the collaboration of members of the Faculty.

By means of studio exercises and discussions, the student is made familiar with the processes of thought and feeling which are basic in design and, as a means to this end, given organized experience in the techniques of graphic expression and in the use of simple tools and materials. The student becomes acquainted with the fundamental concepts of space, form, and function, and the primary structural relationships by which these are expressed and controlled. The properties of materials are analyzed — their structures, surface qualities, plasticities, colors and characteristic forms — and applied as elements in patterns. A study of color and light, and the effects of these upon the perception of form and space, is included.

Architectural Sciences 3a may be accepted as the equivalent of *Design I.*

PLANNING I. *Monday, Wednesday, and Friday, 2–5, and additional hours.* Fall and spring terms. Professors FROST, POND and PERKINS, with the collaboration of members of the Faculty.

An intensive study of topography at the beginning of the fall term is followed by problems concerned with the development of useful patterns in space and structure, based on the correlation and interpretation of social, economic, and physical data. By means of pro-

[26]

DESCRIPTIONS OF COURSES

gressive experience in the solution of problems the student will be made familiar with the methods of the planner, the architect, and the landscape architect, in the preparation of documents and drawings.

Normally, students in *Planning I* must take concurrently *Construction I*. *Architectural Sciences 10* may be accepted under certain conditions as the equivalent of *Planning I*.

CONSTRUCTION I. *Monday and Wednesday, at 12, and Friday, 10–1.* Fall and spring terms. Associate Professor PETER, Assistant Professor NEWTON, and Assistant Professor ULLMAN, with the collaboration of other members of the Faculty.

By means of lectures, conferences, and class exercises, a survey of land areas, services, and uses is followed by a consideration of structures and materials. Lectures deal first with principles, second with facts, third with design expression. Lectures are supplemented by reports requiring the students to make trips of investigation. Classroom work consists of exercises illustrating problems considered in lectures.

Except by special permission, this course is open only to those who present satisfactory evidence of preparation in topography.

Construction I must be taken, normally, concurrently with *Planning I*. *Architectural Sciences 11* may be accepted as the equivalent of *Construction I*.

II

Courses offered by the Department of Architecture

ARCHITECTURE 2b. Architectural Design and Building Construction. *Criticisms on Monday, Wednesday and Friday, 2–6.* Fall and spring terms. Assistant Professor BURCHARD and Mr. HARKNESS, with the collaboration of Associate Professor PETER.

The study of design for buildings and for their sites is integrated by means of a series of special problems of long and short duration. The long problems (four to eight weeks) are case studies of specific projects; the short problems (one day to two weeks) augment these by providing a concentration of interest on some aspect of the longer problems. The social and economic factors underlying design are constantly considered. The designing of buildings is carried on simultaneously with the theoretic study afforded by *Architecture 6*. One of the long problems each year is given in collaboration with instructors in city and regional planning.

[27]

GRADUATE SCHOOL OF DESIGN

ARCHITECTURE 2C. Architectural Design. *Monday to Friday, inclusive, 2–6, and additional hours. Criticisms on Monday, Wednesday and Friday, 2–6. Also morning discussions (8 to 10 times a term) on technical and formal problems and on the contemporary developments in architecture and art.* Associate Professor BOGNER and Associate Professor STUBBINS, with the collaboration of Associate Professor PETER.

In each term there are two long problems and two or more short examination problems. One of the long problems is given in collaboration with instructors in regional planning.

The emphasis of this course is to develop the student's capacity for independent decision and to build up competence in the integration of formal, technical, economic and general human factors. To facilitate the student's approach in design and to make it direct and creative, the physical planning of each problem is preceded by a diagrammatic study of the functions. The problems closely follow the actual practice of the architect-designer by introducing clients, contractors and authorities concerned. Preparation of the programs (clients' requirements) form part of the student's experience. At least one of the long problems calls for a set of execution drawings.

ARCHITECTURE 2d. Architectural Design and Planning. *Criticisms on Monday, Wednesday and Friday afternoons.* Professor GROPIUS and Assistant Professor CURRIE, with the collaboration of other members of the Faculty.

Open only to students who have received the degree *Bachelor of Architecture* from Harvard University or from another university or scientific school approved by the Department Council. Students enrolled in this course are expected to give all of their time to the work of the course.

This work will comprise major problems in architectural design and planning. Four such problems are offered each year. These problems will include: (a) the research necessary for the gathering of social and economic data; (b) the detailing of structural elements and of installation; (c) the computation of financing and of operational cost of buildings; and (d) the study of professional practice (specifications, documents, legal problems).

A student in *Architecture 2d* may not take more than six major problems, four of which must be satisfactory to a jury of the Faculty. In addition, each student may have to complete minor problems satisfactorily. No student may drop a problem without permission of the instructor in charge. For admission to *Architecture 2* see page 17.

[28]

DESCRIPTIONS OF COURSES

ARCHITECTURE 3. Graphics in Theory and Practice; its application to design principles. *Tuesday and Thursday, 2–5.* Spring term. Professor FROST and Assistant Professor LFBOUTILLIER.

By means of lectures, discussions and studio exercises, the student is made familiar with the principles of descriptive geometry and their graphic application in the various forms of projection drawing, including the casting of shadows with the sun chart.

Architectural Sciences 3b may be accepted as the equivalent of *Architecture 3.*

ARCHITECTURE 4b. Architectural Engineering. *Monday, Wednesday and Friday, 9–12.* Fall and spring terms. Associate Professor PETER.

The course is devoted to the study of the principles of architectural engineering and their application all through the course to practical building design. The student's entire time in the classroom is given to working out in conference with the instructor many problems in wood, steel, masonry and concrete structures, such as beams, columns, plate girders, trusses, foundations, retaining walls, etc.

Architecture 4b is open to those only who have passed satisfactorily *Engineering Sciences 7a* or an equivalent course. (See p. 17.)

ARCHITECTURE 4d. Construction Problem. *Two weeks, spring term.* Associate Professor PETER.

At some time during the spring term, the hours ordinarily devoted to design will be given to the development of working drawings and details from a design made in a design course or to computations or to framing drawings.

ARCHITECTURE 4e. Practical Experience in Building Construction. Professor GROPIUS and Associate Professor PETER.

Each candidate for the degree *Bachelor of Architecture* or *Master in Architecture* is required to submit evidence satisfactory to the Council of having completed not less than one term of practical field experience in building construction. This experience is a prerequisite to admission to *Architecture 2d.* All students are expected to obtain employment with an architect, a building authority or a contractor for a period of at least one term, and this employment should consist of work at building sites and in contact with processes of construction.

First-year students and other students entering the Department of Architecture for the first time, and students in Harvard College who expect to enter the Department, are advised to consult Professor PETER in reference to these requirements.

[29]

GRADUATE SCHOOL OF DESIGN

ARCHITECTURE 5b. Mechanical Equipment of Buildings. *Tuesday and Thursday, 9–10.* Fall term. Mr. KNOWLES.

A course of lectures based on a brief survey of the physics and chemistry of air, water, fuels and combustion. Characteristics of materials used in building equipment and insulation. Selection, design, installation and operation of heating and ventilation equipment for steam, hot water, warm air heating, domestic water heating, radiant heating, water supply systems, waste and soil piping, plumbing fixtures, sewage and waste disposal, electric supply, building wiring and lighting design. Inspection is made of typical building installations.

ARCHITECTURE 6. Building Techniques and Professional Practice. *Tuesday, 2–5.* Fall and spring terms. Professor BOGNER.

The principles of the planning of buildings; the development of sites for building purposes; professional practice. This course supplements the work on design problems (*Architecture 2b*).

The study of the planning of buildings is based on an analysis of the function of various building types. The reasons for the architectural forms are traced through a study of the physiological and psychological needs of man, social and economic factors, and the technical considerations which arise in building. The design of buildings is also discussed in reference to health and safety, comfort and convenience, the effect of neighborhoods on the development of building sites, and costs, income and financing. Standards for planning of buildings as contained in the data prepared by government agencies, private organizations, business, industry or individual authorities are reviewed and changes in conditions which indicate trends of progress are pointed out.

The course includes a study of professional practice and of the architect's responsibilities; i.e., the procedure followed in the execution of building projects, the preparation of architectural documents, the architect's position in relation to clients and contractors, and the influence of building legislation.

HISTORY OF ARCHITECTURE 1a (Fine Arts 3A). Architecture in Ancient Times. *Tuesday, Thursday and Saturday, at 10.* Fall term. Professor CONANT.

A descriptive and critical account of European architecture from its origins in Assyria and Egypt to the end of the sixth century. The larger part of the course is devoted to an analysis by a functional method of characteristic structures in Egypt, Greece and Rome.

[30]

DESCRIPTIONS OF COURSES

HISTORY OF ARCHITECTURE 1b (Fine Arts 4A). Mediaeval Architecture. *Tuesday, Thursday and Saturday, at 10.* Spring term. Professor CONANT.

A descriptive and critical account of European architecture from the sixth to the sixteenth century. Beginning with Early Christian architecture, the course continues with a study of Byzantine and Romanesque, and then of the Gothic, from its origin in the Ile-de-France to the beginning of the Renaissance. The greater part of the course will be devoted to the monastery and cathedral; but civil, domestic and military buildings, and the pattern of mediaeval towns, will also be studied; and the course will include an introduction to the decorative arts of sculpture, mosaic and glass-painting.

HISTORY OF ARCHITECTURE 1c (Fine Arts 5A). Renaissance and Baroque Architecture. *Tuesday, Thursday and Saturday, at 11.* Fall term. Professor CONANT.

A descriptive and critical account of European architecture from the early fifteenth century to the late eighteenth century. Beginning with the revival of antique art in Italy, the course covers the architecture of the Renaissance, the Baroque and Rococo, in Italy, Spain, France, England and Germany, and closes on the eve of the modern imitative movements, the neo-classic and the romantic.

HISTORY OF ARCHITECTURE 1d (Fine Arts 7A). Modern Architecture. *Tuesday, Thursday and Saturday, at 11.* Spring term. Professor CONANT.

A descriptive and critical account of European and American architecture from the middle of the eighteenth century to our own time. The course will include, first, a study of nineteenth-century architecture: the decline of the Renaissance tradition; the new classicism at the beginning of the century; the revival of the mediaeval ideal that followed; and the period of eclecticism from 1860 to the Great War of 1914. This will be followed by an account of that search for a new architecture which began in the last quarter of the century in Germany, France and America, and which continues today.

HISTORY OF ARCHITECTURE 1e (Fine Arts 7B). American Architecture. *Tuesday, Thursday and Saturday, at 11.* Summer term. Professor CONANT.

The main outline of this course is like that of Course 7A except that it begins with a short account of the architecture of Ancient America, and of Spanish and English colonial architecture. The European developments which underlie nineteenth- and twentieth-century

[31]

PART THREE

GENERAL INFORMATION

The Programs of Instruction in architecture, landscape architecture, city and regional planning at Harvard University are under the charge of the *Faculty of Design*, composed of all the professors, associate professors and assistant professors who give instruction in these programs. The chief executive officer of this Faculty is the *Dean*, who is responsible for the proper preparation and conduct of its business. The President of the University and the Dean are, *ex officio*, members of the Faculty.

The Faculty has delegated to three *departments* the immediate supervision of the instruction in each of the three fields in its charge. These are the Departments of Architecture, of Landscape Architecture and of Regional Planning. Together these departments form the Graduate School of Design. Each department has an administrative head, the *Chairman*, and a *Council* composed of all the instructors in the field under the supervision of the department.

The Academic Year

The Academic Year is divided for convenience in administration into two terms.

The opening date for each term, together with other data, is announced in the Academic Calendar. This is published annually and is available at the office of the Secretary.

History of the School

The first instruction in architecture at Harvard University was given by Charles Eliot Norton, whose lectures as early as

[38]

GENERAL INFORMATION

1874 included a descriptive and critical account of the history of architecture. In the winter of 1893–94 Professor H. Langford Warren, who was to become the first dean of the Faculty of Architecture, gave courses in the history of Greek and Roman architecture, the success of which was so immediate that in the following year courses in mediaeval architecture, architectural design and drawing were added. These were included in the curriculum of the Lawrence Scientific School, an undergraduate division of the University.

In 1895 a program was outlined which was intended as a complete academic training for architects. Courses in engineering and in graphics were added to those mentioned above and the whole was organized into a studied sequence which included of course such liberal studies as seemed appropriate. The degree *S.B. in Architecture* was awarded to students who completed this program.

In 1900, for the first time in any American university, a professional course in landscape architecture was offered and shortly afterwards a four-year program leading to the degree *S.B. in Landscape Architecture* was established. In 1903 the Charles Eliot Professorship in Landscape Architecture was created.

In 1906 the instruction in both architecture and landscape architecture was placed upon a graduate basis and professional degrees in these fields were established. In 1912 the Schools of Architecture and of Landscape Architecture were organized as a separate division of the University under the Faculty of the Graduate Schools of Applied Science. In 1914 the Faculty of Architecture was created and given entire control over the curricula and degrees of the two Schools.

Since 1909 the subject of city planning had been taught in the School of Landscape Architecture by Professor James Sturgis Pray. In 1923 there was established in this School an optional curriculum leading to a degree which was especially designated as a degree in city planning. In 1929 the Charles

GRADUATE SCHOOL OF DESIGN

Dyer Norton Professorship in Regional Planning was founded and shortly afterwards a separate School of City Planning was organized and placed, like the Schools of Architecture and Landscape Architecture, under the control of the Faculty of Architecture.

In 1935 these three schools were united to form the present Graduate School of Design.

NOTES

1 Harvard Architects and the Bauhaus Ethos

1. As is well known, László Moholy-Nagy accepted a similar invitation to Chicago, followed by Ludwig Mies van der Rohe, to begin what eventually became the Chicago Institute of Design of the Illinois Institute of Technology.

2. "Walter Gropius et son école/Walter Gropius: The Spread of an Idea," *Architecture d'Aujourd'hui*, Special Issue, February 1950.

3. "GENETRIX: Personal Contributions to American Architecture," *Architectural Review*, Special Issue, May 1957.

4. Peter Blake in *The Bulletin of The Museum of Modern Art*, vol. 16, no. 1, 1949, n.p.

5. Marcel Breuer, *Marcel Breuer: Buildings and Projects, 1921–1961* (London: Thames and Hudson, 1962), p. 214.

6. Willy Boesiger, ed., *Le Corbusier et Pierre Jeanneret: Oeuvre Complète, 1929–34* (Zurich: Dr. H. Girsberger & Cie, 1935), p. 48.

7. Walter Gropius, "The Architect within our Industrial Society," in *Scope of Total Architecture* (New York: Collier Books, 1962), pp. 77–78; first published as "Gropius Appraises Today's Architect," *Architectural Forum*, May 1952.

8. Victor Lundy, "Art Alone, Untiring, Stays to Us," *AIA Journal*, May 1959, p. 15; Paul Rudolph, "Architectural Education in the U.S.A.," *Zodiac*, vol. 8, June 1961, pp. 162–165; and John Johansen, "John M. Johansen Declares Himself," *Architectural Forum*, January/February 1966, pp. 64–67.

9. Vincent Scully, "Doldrums in the Suburbs," *Perspecta 9/10*, 1965, p. 290.

10. Colin Rowe, "Neoclassicism and Modern Architecture," *Oppositions 1*, 1973, pp. 1–26 (written in 1957).

11. Walter Gropius, "Appraisal of the Development of Modern Architecture," in *Scope of Total Architecture*, p. 59; first published as "The Formal and Technical Problems of Modern Architecture and Planning," *Journal R.I.B.A.*, May 19, 1934.

12. Ibid.

13. A far more controversial tall building with a two-dimensional top is Johnson's AT&T building, judging from the media attention it commands (the latest at this writing being the report of a benefit/*haute-volée* auction of its architectural model in the *New York Times*, January 12, 1982). Although the AT&T building, will stand pressed against similar new and tall buildings in midtown Manhattan, its standard portrayal in the press is as an isolated object that can be viewed from afar.

14. One is reminded of the axiom from E. H. Gombrich's "Meditations on a Hobby Horse or the Roots of Artistic Form": "The greater the wish to ride the fewer may be the features that will do for a horse." (L. L. Whyte, ed., *Aspects of Form*, Bloomington: Indiana University Press, 1951, p. 218.)

15. Francis Bacon, "Of Counsell," in *Essays*, World's Classics (New York: Oxford University Press, 1940), p. 89 (essay 20).

2 Buildings

16. In most of the literature on Johnson's work, another museum, the Amon Carter Museum of Western Art, 1961, is mentioned as a modern mutation of Schinkel's Altes Museum. Yet the entrance sequence of the Sheldon Memorial Art Gallery makes it at least as worthy a comparison and in a sense a more eloquent one.

17. A positive example, illustrating almost identical points and having a similar spatial program and image context, would be Terragni's Casa del Fascio, Como, 1932–1936. For an illustrated discussion, see Peter Eisenman, "Casa del Fascio," *Perspecta 13/14*, 1971, pp. 62–65; and Panos Koulermos, "Terragni, Lingeri, and Italian Rationalism," *Architectural Design* March 1962, pp. 112–115.

18. In the built version the situation is somewhat ameliorated by the differentiation of the lobby entry as clearly major.

19. This section is based on an article I coauthored with Alan Chimacoff, "Two Cornell Professors: 'A Promise Unfulfilled,'" *The Cornell Daily Sun* (Ithaca, N.Y.), May 4, 1973. The piece was written in celebration of the museum's inauguration two days before.

20. Ada Louise Huxtable, "Pei's Bold Gem: Cornell Museum," *New York Times*, June 11, 1973. (Almost all of Pei's public buildings have received favorable *Times* reviews.)

21. The original dimensions of the University of Virginia Great Lawn, before it was extended to the south and closed off by Stanford White in 1898, were approximately 250 by 750 feet.

22. Part of that neoclassical veneer, and it is scarcely more than that, results from the requirement that *all* structures, including the platform, be faced with the same grayish-brown brick, infusing the whole with the excitement of a Brooks Brothers suit.

23. Calling this covered pedestrian way an arcade greatly injures the concept of arcade by substituting a name full of humanistic associations for the actual thing. The process of inflation of values, so typical of much contemporary

architecture, often begins with such a discrepancy between name and fact and results in the eventual destruction of the original concept.

3 Teaching

24. "Site Development for Family Residences," Master's Class problem, 1951.

25. Ibid.

26. Ibid.

27. Leonardo Benevolo, *History of Modern Architecture* (Cambridge, Mass.: The MIT Press, 1971), pp. 652–653.

28. "A Public Library for Cambridge," Arch 2d problem, given by "Professor Gropius and Mr. Thompson," 2/6/50, "Judgement" 3/31/50.

29. "An Art Center," Arch 2d problem, given by "Walter Gropius and William W. Lyman, Jr.," 11/24/47, "Jury" 1/29/48.

30. Ibid.

31. Scully, "Doldrums in the Suburbs," p. 283.

32. "An Elementary School for Oak Hill Park, Newton, Massachusetts," Master's Class problem, 1948/49. Moholy-Nagy, in his foreword to *The New Vision*, The New Bauhaus Books, ed. Walter Gropius and László Moholy-Nagy, no. 1 (New York: W. W. Norton & Co., Inc., 1938), expresses a similar idea: "To reach this objective . . . the closest connection between art, science and technology . . . one of the problems of Bauhaus education is to keep alive in grown-ups the child's sincerity of emotion, his truth of observation, his fantasy and his creativeness."

33. Walter Gropius et al., *The Architects Collaborative Inc., 1945 to 1965* (New York: Architectural Book Publishing Co., 1966), p. 20.

34. Gropius, *Scope of Total Architecture*, p. 59.

35. Ibid., p. 12.

36. Ibid., p. 54.

37. Catalog of the Graduate School of Design, Harvard University, 1946–1947, p. 28.

38. Ibid.

39. "A Graduate Center for Harvard University," Master's Class problem, 1948.

40. "A New Celtic Tower," *Architectural Forum*, November 1958, pp. 127–131.

41. Unfortunately, no illustrations of student work produced in the GSD preliminary course, "Design I: Theory and Practice of Design," were available for this essay. All we have is the 1946–1947 catalog's description of intent:

"By means of studio exercises and discussions the student is made familiar with the processes of thought and feeling which are basic in design. . . . The properties of materials are analyzed—their structures, surface qualities, plasticities, colors and characteristic forms—are applied as elements in patterns."

42. Moholy-Nagy, *The New Vision*, foreword, p. 6.

43. Gropius, "Blueprint of an Architect's Education," in *Scope of Total Architecture*, p. 53; previously published as "Training the Architect," *Twice A Year* (New York), no. 2, 1939; and "Plan pour un enseignement de l'Architecture," *Architecture d'Aujourd'hui*, February 1950.

44. Ibid.

45. Ibid., passim.

46. Ibid., p. 51.

Addendum to Note 6

Although the Errazuris house (figures 2, 3, 7, 9, 10, and 11) was described by Le Corbusier as a built project, other sources indicate that it was, in fact, never built.

ILLUSTRATION CREDITS

1. Author.

2. From Willy Boesiger, ed., *Le Corbusier et Pierre Jean-neret: Oeuvre Complète*, 1929–34 (Zurich: Dr. H. Girs-berger & Cie., 1935), pp. 48–49.

3. After architect's drawing in Boesiger, *Le Corbusier, 1929–34*, p. 48.

4. Photo: Ezra Stoller. From Peter Blake, *Marcel Breuer: Architect and Designer* (New York: The Museum of Modern Art, 1949), p. 111.

5. Plans from Blake, *Marcel Breuer*, p. 110; section from *Architectural Forum*, May 1949, p. 97.

6. Photo: Ezra Stoller. From Blake, *Marcel Breuer*, p. 112.

7. From Boesiger, *Le Corbusier, 1929–34*, p. 51.

8. From Marcel Breuer, *Marcel Breuer: Buildings and Projects, 1921–1961* (London: Thames and Hudson, 1962), p. 214.

9, 10. From Boesiger, *Le Corbusier, 1929–34*, p. 51, 52.

11. Author.

12. Photo: Ben Schnall, from *Architectural Review*, May 1957.

13. From *Architectural Record*, May 1957, p. 142.

14. Photo: Robert Damora. From *Architectural Record*, May 1958, p. 170.

15. From *Architectural Record*, May 1958, p. 170.

16. Photos: Ezra Stoller. From Walter Gropius et al., *The Architects Collaborative Inc., 1945 to 1965* (New York: Architectural Book Publishing Co., 1966), p. 46.

17. From Gropius et al., *The Architects Collaborative Inc.*, p. 38.

18. Photo: Alexandre Georges. From Philip Johnson, *Philip Johnson: Architecture 1949–65* (New York: Holt, Rinehart and Winston, 1966), p. 37.

19. From Johnson, *Philip Johnson, 1949–65*, p. 36.

20. Photo: Ezra Stoller. From *Architectural Forum*, June 1951, p. 157.

21. From *Architectural Forum*, June 1951, p. 157.

22. Photo: Ezra Stoller. From *Architectural Record*, May 1958, p. 88.

23. From *Architectural Record*, May 1958, p. 98.

24, 25. From *Architectural Forum*, 1950, p. 91.

26. Photo: Vince Lisanti. From *Architectural Record*, May 1958, p. 88.

27. From *Architectural Record*, 1958, p. 88.

28. From Willy Boesiger and Oscar Stonorov, eds., *Le Corbusier et Pierre Jeanneret: Oeuvre Complète, 1910–29* (Zurich: Dr. H. Girsberger & Cie., 1930), p. 49.

29. From Boesiger and Stonorov, *Le Corbusier, 1910–29*, p. 48.

30, 31. From Boesiger and Stonorov, *Le Corbusier, 1910–29*, p. 49.

32. Author.

33. The Metropolitan Museum of Art, New York.

34. Photo: T. Reynold Williams. From Colin Rowe and Fred Koetter, *Collage City* (Cambridge, Mass.: MIT Press, 1978), p. 152.

35. Photo: David Franzen. From *Process Architecture*, vol. 8, 1979, p. 135.

36. From *Process Architecture*, vol. 8, 1979, p. 132.

37. Photo: Author.

38. Photo: Richard Payne. From Nory Miller, *Johnson/Burgee Architecture* (New York: Random House, 1979), p. 106.

39. From *Process Architecture*, vol. 8, 1979, p. 133.

40. After architects' drawings.

41. Author.

42. From the *New York Times*, January 17, 1969.

43–45. Photo: Author.

46, 47. Author.

48. Plans from H. and M. Gullichsen, Villa Mairea visitors' pamphlet, about 1972. Section: Author.

49. Author.

50, 51. Photo: Author.

52, 53. From August Grisbach, *Karl Friedrich Schinkel* (Leipzig: Insel-Verlag, 1924), pp. 81–82.

54, 55. Photos: Ezra Stoller. From Johnson, *Architecture*, pp. 88–89.

56. After National Geographic Survey Map.

57. From Johnson, *Architecture*, p. 86.

58. After *Progressive Architecture*, November 1981, p. 87.

59, 60. From Grisbach, *Schinkel*, pp. 83, 89.

61. Author.

62–64. From Gropius et al., *Architects Collaborative Inc.*, pp. 222–223.

65, 66. From *Architecture for the Arts: The State University of New York College at Purchase* (New York: The Museum of Modern Art, 1971), pp. 32–33.

67, 68. From *Casabella,* October 1965, pp. 70–71.

69, 70. From *Architecture for the Arts,* pp. 24–25.

71. Photo: Ezra Stoller. From *Process Architecture,* vol. 8, 1979, p. 56.

72. From *Process Architecture,* vol. 8, 1979, pp. 62–63.

73. Photos: Louis Checkman. From *Architectural Forum,* May 1968, p. 67.

74–76. From *Architectural Forum,* May 1968, p. 68.

77. From *Architectural Forum,* November 1969, pp. 80–81.

78–80. From *Architecture Plus,* August 1973, pp. 23–24.

81. Photo: Author.

82, 83. From *Architectural Design,* October 1965, pp. 493–494.

84. From *Architecture Plus,* August 1973, p. 20.

85. From *Architectural Design,* October 1965, p. 494.

86. From *Architecture Plus,* August 1973, p. 19.

87. After the architects' drawing in *Architectural Review,* January 1963, p. 13.

88, 89. From *Architectural Review,* January 1963, p. 12.

90–92. From *Architectural Design,* October 1965, pp. 495, 499.

93. After the architects' drawing in *Domus,* September 1963, p. 7.

94. From the Cornell University prospectus on continuing education (Ithaca, N.Y.: Cornell University, 1974.)

95. Photos: Office of University Publications and the Herbert F. Johnson Museum of Art, Cornell University, Ithaca, New York.

96. From *A Guide to the Herbert F. Johnson Museum of Art* (Ithaca, N.Y.: Cornell University, May 1973).

97. From Mario Morini, *Atlante di Storia dell'Urbanistica* (Milan, 1963), p. 109.

98. From *Architecture for the Arts,* p. 17.

99. From F. D. Nichols, *Thomas Jefferson's Architectural Drawings* (Chapel Hill: University of North Carolina Press, 1957), fig. 26.

100. Photo: Ralph Thompson, courtesy University of Virginia Information Service, Charlottesville.

101. Photo: Courtesy of University of Virginia Information Service, Charlottesville.

102. Photo: Louis Checkman. From *Architecture for the Arts,* p. 15.

103. Photo: George Cserna.

104. From *Architecture for the Arts,* p. 9.

105. Author.

106. From Hans Wingler, *Bauhaus* (Cambridge, Mass.: MIT Press, 1969), p. 489.

107. Photo: Robert Burke. From Vincent Scully, *American Architecture and Urbanism* (New York: Praeger, 1969), p. 184.

108. Author.

109. From Herbert Bayer, Walter Gropius, and Ise Gropius, eds., *Bauhaus: 1919–1928* (New York: The Museum of Modern Art, 1938), p. 124.

110. Photo: Norman McGrath. From *Architectural Forum,* August/September 1964, p. 145.

111. From *Architectural Forum,* August/September 1964, p. 145.

112, 113. Photos: Ezra Stoller. From Robert A. M. Stern, *New Directions in American Architecture* (New York: George Braziller, 1969), pp. 38–39.

114. Photo: Nathaniel Liberman. From *Architectural Forum,* January/February 1973, p. 34.

115. From *Architectural Forum,* January/February 1973, p. 34.

116, 117. From Walter Gropius, *Scope of Total Architecture* (New York: Collier Books, 1962), following p. 64.

118. After G. C. Manson, *Frank Lloyd Wright to 1910* (New York: Reinhold, 1958), p. 7.

119. From Mary P. M. Sekler, "The Early Drawings of Charles Edouard Jeanneret (Le Corbusier), 1902–1908" (Ph.D. dissertation, Harvard University, 1973), fig. 74, no. 39.

120. From Gullichsen, *Villa Mairea* visitors' pamphlet.